I'M DYIN' HERE

A LIFE IN THE PAPER

TIM GROBATY

Brown Paper Press
Long Beach, CA

Brown Paper Press

6475 E. Pacific Highway, #329
Long Beach, CA 90803

Cover by Evan Backes
Interior by Gary A. Rosenberg

Library of Congress Control Number: 2015954708

ISBN: 978-1-941932-06-3 (print)
978-1-941932-07-0 (ebook)

10 9 8 7 6 5 4 3 2 1

*For Rich Archbold & the Memory of
Larry Allison, newspapermen.*

Contents

The paper—that daily report on the idiocy and the brilliance of the species—had never before missed an appointment. Now it was gone.

—TOM RACHMAN, *THE IMPERFECTIONISTS*

Introduction

I am. I am dying here. Ask my doctor. "Tim," he says to me, after first asking if I'm still working for that rag of a newspaper, which I am and at which admission he shakes his head slowly and doctorly. He says, "You're at the age where your body is going to be changing in many ways. All of them bad."

Jesus, Doc, break it to me gently. How about, "Grandma's on the roof," or "While some people die quickly and painlessly . . . "

Ah, but who cares? Doesn't bother me. I cleave to the childlike notion that death isn't a law of nature; it's merely a theory. Everyone dies? You got proof of that? There are more than 7 billion people right now who haven't died. My inner oddsmaker tells me that even if 99.9 percent of these people die, more than 7 million of them will continue to feel fine forever. So there's that I have going for me.

On the downside, I am a journalist. Specifically, a newspaper columnist. And it's not a theory that all newspapers will die. It's a law. It can't not happen. I'm at the stage of a long career where my job is going to be changing in many ways. All of them bad. We don't buy ink by the barrel these days. We pick up a half-gallon on the way to work.

So, yeah, as a print journalist? Dead as a bobbin boy, dead as a scrivener, dead as a whorehouse pianna-player—so many occupations that once sustained this glorious world.

Thank Christ I'm not twenty-one, the age I was when I started earning a paycheck in the journalism business. I picked the right era to turn sixty. Journalism paid me good enough money back in the years before raises were outlawed in the American workplace. Enough to buy a house in the suburbs and raise a pair of children, Ray and Hannah, both in their twenties (all this done, of course, with my wife Jane's biological assistance and supplementary salary, which in the early years was considerably less than mine before we swapped trouser-wearing roles about halfway through our respective careers. She works for the city. We'll always have cities). My young friends and colleagues now come into the field with an equal amount of enthusiasm and zeal as I did forty years ago, but with a certain amount of dread as well, knowing that if they ever hope to buy a home they will (barring a glorious inheritance) likely have to go into a different and more dream-crushing line of work.

So, for once, I timed something right: my birth. Though I might've miscalculated by six or seven years. We'll have to see. We'll have to see which one of us dies first: me or my profession.

I was born where I did almost everything else in my life, in Long Beach, CA, with the help of the doctors and nuns at St. Mary's Hospital (today it is a "Medical Center." I presume they still deign to take in the odd baby delivery).

If I collapsed at work, and assuming someone bothered to call an ambulance, I would be whisked a half-mile away, back to St. Mary's. Google assures me the ambulance could get me from work to hospital in three minutes. Worst-case scenario, my life would end up in a tidy little circle, like a neatly written story, with the end echoing the beginning.

A lot's happened to me since the day I was born, which is how I'm managing to get a good part of a book written. Among the first things was my mom died. About fifty years later, my second mom died, then, for God's sake, my third mom—my favorite, my grandmother—died. In an attempt to balance the population scales, my wife and I have two children, and we all of us live, went to school, and work in Long Beach.

I don't have a long employment resume. I was a student assistant at a high-poverty-level school teaching—get a load of this—algebra (the hilarity will hit you later), I worked at my granddad's tuxedo shop, I painted a fence or two and some houses, I worked at a steakhouse in a swank part of town, and I clerked, or customer-serviced, at RadioShack, the only place I ever worked where I had to wear a tie.

In terms of journalism, I wrote for a huge newspaper with several hundred employees who filled up a five-story building in downtown Long Beach; I worked for a mid-size newspaper on the top floor of an oceanfront high-rise where I could see a good stretch of California's coastline from my desk; and I've worked at a smallish newspaper in a revamped storefront on Pine across the street from a little food mart run by a guy named Vijay.

All those newspapers were the *Press-Telegram*.

CHAPTER ONE

"Journalism," I Said

Here's a brace of hilarious clichés that totally pertain to me:

One, I Am Married to the Sea (or: The Sea Is a Fickle Mistress). I love the ocean (that's why I married it, or made it my mistress) and everything about it except the math and the occasional terror. In high school I had the greatest living marine biology teacher, a recovering Marine and a genius of oceanic proportions. I spent weekends in my youth searching for new (to me) species of mollusks in tide pools from Point Conception to the Mexican border. My dream was to someday become a marine biologist. Something along the lines of Doc Ricketts of *Cannery Row*. (Doc was a real person, and he wrote the bible of my enthusiasm, *Between Pacific Tides*.)

Two, Music Is My Life. I grew up in the best era of rock and roll, and I studied it fervently from the time

I could toddle. I bought the Byrds' "Turn! Turn! Turn!" LP when I was ten, bought a guitar when I was fifteen, played around in a few high school and college bands, and caught every concert I could afford. I dreamed of being a rock star. Nothing serious. Something along the lines of a Jackson Browne would've be sufficient. (Jackson was a real person, and he wrote the soundtrack of my angst-ridden late teen years, *Late for the Sky*.)

Here's the thing. I mentioned math, which is also what my college counselor mentioned when he begged me to leave science to people who at least had a glancing knowledge of numbers. I was especially bad at algebra. I like letters, but I didn't see any place for them in mathematics. I still have no idea what $x - y$ equals. I'm gonna guess z, but I can't show my work. My dream of being a marine biologist was finished.

Music? Deader, even. There, again, it was simply a matter of ability, including math, which rears its addled head when it comes to music theory. I could amuse and occasionally amaze myself, but I couldn't find anyone else to share my wonderment. After a few public performances, I limited my playing and singing to my children until they were old enough to say "quit it." I was, and I swear this is true, kicked out of a band called The Grobatys, and it wasn't a family band. I was the only Grobaty in it. The rest of the band members just thought it was a funny name. We all had a good laugh, but then they said, "Yeah, but seriously, you have to leave." Happily, the band didn't go on to be a huge success, which would have made me the Pete Best of The Grobatys.

My college counselor paged through his Big Book of Careers, throwing out all the things you need math for: things like astronomy, physics, chemistry—the obvious stuff, but also vocations like taxidermy, culinary arts, air-conditioning repair, or running any kind of business in which money is exchanged. It was getting desperate. I couldn't handle the math that was required to be a cab driver.

"Ah, here we go," our counselor said peering over the lenses of his pince-nez (as I recall). "Radio or Journalism. Pick one."

I liked the idea of radio because it would allow me to foist my musical taste on what was bound to be my fawning listenership, but being on-air made me nervous. I don't like being in front of people. At all. I'm not even happy about the idea of you staring at this page. And while you can argue that being on the radio doesn't entail being in front of people *per se*, I would know that they're out there, listening to me like I'm an idiot and that they'd somehow be able to tell that to make myself at ease I was imagining them all sitting around with no clothes on.

"Journalism," I said.

So, I show up in the journalism trailer at Long Beach City College, a school that had sturdy, pre-war lath-and-plaster classrooms for every other subject, and a tin mobile home for its journalists, like it was just going to be a passing fad subject.

The editor-in-chief of the school newspaper said to the new students, "Gather over here if you want to write news, and over there if you want to write features."

Another fork in the road forcing me to make an uneducated guess about which way to go. I thought newspapers just had news and movie theaters had features. I seriously didn't have any idea what a feature was.

"What's a feature?" I asked an editor who buried his head in his hand and chewed madly on a pencil, like, "Why does that counselor with the pince-nez keep sending me these people?"

He blathered on about the difference: Your news reporter will go out on the scene and cover things ranging from government meetings to murders, while your features writer will do profiles of notable people, or maybe even a column of some sort.

Like music? I could do a music column? I'll take features. "I want to be a columnist."

Not so fast. There were dues to be paid. "We'll start you out doing some small stories and see how that works," said the editor, and I don't recall the very first story I did, but I remember the last line, which wrapped up many of my earliest pieces for the *Viking:*

"Punch and cookies will be served."

Dues-paying on my march to college-paper columnist was too painful to recall. Little calendar items, school dances, probably something about some sort of carnival that included three-legged races between sororities and fraternities. The Spring Sing.

I wrote a first-person story about participating in a disaster drill at Long Beach Airport, in which I played a compelling role as a guy suffering with burns and open wounds. My editors loved it. My grandmother hated it because there was a picture of me with the story that made it look like I was dead—a shout-out here to the disaster drill makeup team from the drama department.

From out of my own ashes, I rose to become a columnist after that story. I was instantly famous on a community-college level, recognized in certain areas of the quad and occasionally as far afield as the Student Union.

I had reached the pinnacle of my collegiate profession, and sat in the office at the *Viking*, whacking the keys of my typewriter, expounding on such topics as underserved night-schoolers, rabbits on campus, and the idiocy of one of the guys running for student body president (I believe I called the candidate "dumber than 40 monkeys locked in a room")—a column which irritated the journalism adviser to the extent that he offered to help the candidate file a libel suit against me. That was real nice.

I planned to expand my readership that I developed at City College by enrolling at Cal State Long Beach, but I was fizzling out in college life. I went to all of my classes once and had one story in the university's *Daily 49er* newspaper, and then I dropped out to join the circus.

CHAPTER TWO

Something Shy
of Dustin Hoffman

Journalism was never so robust when I first visited the *Press-Telegram*. It was 1976, the year *All the President's Men* was released and suddenly everyone wanted to uncover corruption and crime, handsomely, like Robert Redford, Dustin Hoffman, and Jason Robards.

It was at that time that I waltzed—yes, waltzed, such was the lofty and elegant level of my cocksurety—into the deep, walnut-paneled office of the *Press-Telegram*'s editor and generously offered to be a columnist for the publication. No resumé at all, just my unassailable reputation and my startlingly good looks.

If visiting my opinion on a couple hundred thousand readers, with said visitation appearing under my name and not uncomely face, would bring a modicum of prestige to the *Press-Telegram*, then, yes, I would be willing to offer my skills, pending amenable salary terms and other incidentals upon which I'm sure we can swiftly agree, being reasonable men—my young Redford–Bob Woodward to the editor's debonair and learned Robards–Ben Bradlee.

The fact that the editor, Larry Allison, didn't smirk, never mind turn crimson with laughter or rage, is a mark of the man's dignity and decorum that I would admire even beyond his death some decades later.

Rather, Mr. Allison explained that if I were to have a job at all at the newspaper, it would be as a copy boy, filling glue pots, running copy up and down stairs, buying booze for the late-night copy editors, and carrying out the wishes and caprices of reporters whose sole jobs, it seemed, were to come up with ever-increasingly demeaning and pointless tasks for me.

"And even that job is in huge demand," continued Allison. "Since this movie came out, we've got people with master's degrees applying for a job as copy boy."

Even so, somehow, with my educational bona fides consisting of something like one fly-tying class shy of an Associate of Arts degrees from a prestigious community college, I got the job of copy boy. Something south of Dustin Hoffman. More like Opie in *The Andy Griffith Show*.

CHAPTER THREE

Glue Pots and the Weather

Clouds ran low along the coast and inland to Sixth Street on an early brisk spring morning in May 1976. It was my first day as a copy boy at the *Independent, Press-Telegram*.

The weather that day is a matter of public record.

I hauled myself into the second-floor newsroom at 6 a.m., tiptoed around a bunch of sleeping copy editors and put on a pot of coffee. I looked at slot man Bill Shelton's Pall Mall filterless cigarette that was clamped between his index and middle finger as he gently snored. He'd be awake soon. He used the cigarette to give himself a five-minute nap. The cherry-red tip would reach his fingers any second, and he'd bolt up with a start and resume his work, writing screamer headlines for the morning street edition.

I scrolled a sheet of newsprint into a typewriter,

slugged it WEATHEREAR 1-1-1-1 ("Ear" is a now-fairly defunct term for the little boxes to the right and left of the masthead. The left ear was usually a brief promo to get you to go inside the paper—TODDLER FOUND. PAGE B-1—and the right ear was my exclusive domain: the weather ear. I mused for a moment, then typed: "Low clouds this morning, otherwise fair through Monday. Highs today and Monday 73. Lows in the upper 50s. Complete weather, Page B-7."

Terse. Paradoxically both sharp and blunt. If it was a style reminiscent of anyone's, it would be Hemingway's. Occasionally I would throw in a gaudy Fitzgeraldian adjective, like "gusty." If things got too gloomy, I could do a Faulkner that would make you afraid to leave the house.

Writing the weather report was the only writing a copy boy did, and it was one of the few moments of respectability in a copy boy's day. Otherwise, I filled gluepots—pages of a news story were glued together into one long sheet in those days before being shot up a pneumatic tube to typesetters. I changed the ribbons and the paper on the wire-service typers that clattered away like boxing tin men in the wire room. I went out daily to buy vodka and gin for the copy editors who always spoke in code, telling us to go across the street to Thrifty to check out "the white goods sale."

I drove hundreds of miles to pick up various documents and photos throughout Southern California. I picked up take-out for reporters and editors. I took managers' cars in for servicing. I picked up wives and job applicants at the airport. I hand-delivered newspapers to subscribers who didn't get their papers. I lugged hundreds of newspapers up hundreds of steep concrete steps from the mailroom every day to sweetly place at the fingertips of editors and reporters. I kept a log of every picture that was in the next day's paper. I tore off wire copy as it came up through the machine, handing the copy to the appropriate editors.

I still can recall jumping up like an eager servant every time news editor Hank Fishbach would yell "Dick!"—the name of some distant predecessor, which was what Fishbach called every copy boy, presumably because he didn't want to spend half the shift learning a new name for each kid who came through that job.

I spent days in the newspaper morgue researching stories for reporters and looking up photos for editors, learning the arcane system of the librarians who spent their days clipping and filing stories from the paper (hippies, coffee-house musicians and poets, anti-war demonstrators could all be found in the folder labeled "Beatniks").

I photocopied magazine pieces that reporters wanted to read without having to go through the hassle of turning magazine pages. These little bastards would make me cut out the ads and just glue the copy onto paper so it would be easier to read. (I will tell you that I spent years crafting and exacting revenge on every single person who wronged me in that course of that debasing, Dickensian job. I had sort of a Black Mass shrine in my basement closet with their names, each crossed off with a near-beatific satisfaction as they were dealt with—usually without knowing why their lives had taken such sudden and misfortunate turns.)

There was no job too small or menial for me, though people who outranked me, which is to say the rest of the 600 or so people who worked at the combined *Independent, Press-Telegram* in 1976 and 1977, never grew tired of looking for one.

"No" was never an option. I was sent to Hollywood to pick up Oscar credentials for a reporter one year and the office was, of course, full of press people all wanting their badges.

The lady whose ghastly job it was to help these reporters couldn't find the name of the reporter whose passes I was supposed to pick up. I told her to keep looking.

"Who the hell are you?" she snapped.

"Me? I'm about a half-dozen notches down from nobody, but if I go back without Oscar passes I might as well keep going to Mexico."

Gratified to know that there was a soul on this earth below her station, she pressed on and found the misfiled credentials.

It was the least glamorous job in journalism, but I came to realize it was a job at which every journalist should start—at least in those days when newspaper buildings were like countries, with dozens of little villages and a few big cities, the natives of which rarely communicated with each other outside of vicious tribal wars.

The copy boy is the unseen little kid, dressed in rags, too young and inexperienced to fight and, as a result, can scamper from village to village, making acquaintances that would be unlikely or unseemly for the more adult villagers. I knew everyone in the pressroom, those ink-covered musclemen who weren't allowed most places in the building lest they muck it up with the ink-sodden soles of their shoes. I knew the grouchy paste-up men and women who could make an attractive doily out of your liver with their X-acto knives should you get on their expansive bad sides. I knew the ladies in the cafeteria who would snap and growl at almost every customer except me. When I complained of a hangover, they'd take me into the kitchen for a shot of Tuaca. I knew the truck drivers and how to sweet-talk them into a couple of gallons of gas from their pump out back. I knew the home-delivery people and the classified ad girls. I could run a paper with who and what I knew after a year or two on the job at the bottom of the hierarchy.

I also knew this: I wasn't going to leave this business. It was too much fun. Even at its worst, it was way too much fun.

CHAPTER FOUR

Fat and Rich

Newspapers worldwide were fat and rich, from the earliest days of print to the 1970s. The print journalism industry could play Falstaff in *Henry V* without even showing up for a table reading.

The *Independent, Press-Telegram,* by the time I arrived, was the only daily newspaper in town. The P-T was an afternoon newspaper, while the *Independent* was the morning paper. In 1952, the papers merged with the unwieldy masthead *Independent, Press-Telegram,* but the Indy was still the name used for the morning editions, while the P-T catered to afternoon and evening readers. The *Independent* was dropped from the paper's name in 1981, and the *P-T* became the morning paper, while the afternoon/ evening edition was dropped altogether.

It was a major metropolitan daily with money enough to lure reporters from the bigger papers in the east who wanted to come to Southern California. We had reporters and editors from the *New York Times,* the *Philadelphia Inquirer,* the *Miami Herald,* and others.

The paper had a huge building and a staff to fill it.

Here's some of what the *Press-Telegram* had on the second floor of Sixth Street and Pine Avenue when I was eating the anchovy sandwiches and leftover lasagna the copy editors were throwing to the copy boy to keep him alive long enough to buy the bedding (booze) across the street:

We had an editor-in-chief in a plush corner office with walnut-paneled walls and a TV. We had a managing editor with his own secretary and a squadron of assistant managing editors. We had night and afternoon city editors to handle the daily local news and deploy the reporters; assistant city editors to help the city editors; a regional editor who dealt with the news from the more far-flung of the twenty-some outlying cities we covered; a Sunday editor who just concentrated on the big paper of the week; a news editor who sorted through state, national, and international news; a wire editor who handled the miscellaneous stories that came across the wire; a slot man (OK, person, but virtually always a man) who assigned stories for the copy editors to read for grammatical and factual errors and write headlines; we had a business editor, a travel editor, a religion editor, a food editor, a TV editor, a society editor, a women's section editor, an assistant women's section editor, an entertainment editor, a dozen or so photographers, a few dozen reporters, a mammoth sports department with writers who covered and traveled with the Dodgers, the Angels, the Rams, the Lakers, Cal State Long Beach, USC, and UCLA.

The Press-Telegram had its own garage staffed by full-time mechanics who worked on the trucks and the fleet of company cars that the reporters used to go on assignment. There were full-time painters, electricians, and carpenters forever redesigning offices.

The paper had too much money and not enough space to store it in. I can recall looking in an Associated Press annual from the early 1970s. These were books that dealt with the issues of the time and problems facing newspapers, and in that particular volume, a great deal of space was given over to the quandary of what newspapers were supposed to do with their awesome profits.

They took their best shot at merely spending it from the top down. Our publisher had a home on the biggest lot in Long Beach as well as pads at St. Andrews in Scotland, in Miami, and on the 17-mile drive near Pebble Beach on the Monterey Peninsula. An indiscreet teller at his bank once told me that he kept a balance of $1 million in his checkbook. Workers got regular raises. When I started reporting, I was paid at the one-year scale rather than the beginner's six-month pay grade. A year later, finding they were losing the money-spending battle, they kicked me up to five-year journeyman pay.

At budget time, editors pleaded with reporters to come up with story ideas that entailed putting them on a plane and flying somewhere. It was as if the money was just ganging up on the newspaper, and editors had to figure out a way to get rid of it before it got all moldy and started rotting at the bottom of the pile.

The newspaper never closed. The front doors were always unlocked. The thundering presses in the basement worked without rest, churning out five editions each day to meet the needs of readers' varied preferences and habits. Some residents were morning readers, some evening readers. Some bought a paper from the rack, wanting the closest we could come to up-to-the-minute news; some bought it on the street after work. And some we just tried to snag with street sales with bigger, sexier headlines than those that came with the more staid home delivery papers.

So, to meet all these needs, and because we had the money to do it, we put out: the *Independent* home edition, the *Independent* street, the early (Metro) *Press-Telegram* street, the later *Press-Telegram* street and the *Press-Telegram* home edition. Circulation was a robust 152,000 on Sunday in 1978, serving a city of about 400,000.

In the early 1980s, the modern high-water mark, there were 143 full-time editors, reporters, and photographers. And a handful of columnists, the Chosen Few, the elite men and women who came and went as they chose (sometimes sober in one direction and not so much in the other), writing about whatever suited their fancy.

CHAPTER FIVE

Welcome to the Club

In 1979, I married Jane, who I met at Long Beach City College. My career was on wobbly legs. You don't get married on a copy boy's salary, but we went off to our honeymoon in Hawaii with the assurance from the paper's Sunday editor that when I returned to work, I would be promoted to a reporter.

The Sunday editor gave me my first leg up by giving me an entire page to fill with rock-and-roll news and reviews while I was still a copy boy. On the page opposite mine, the regional editor, Harold Glicken, was given a page to fill with movie reviews. He was my chief mentor, dragging me up to be his sole reporter for a new section called Neighbors, writing light features: the guy on the block who fixes kids' bikes for free; the lady who grew a seventeen-pound zucchini; a crossing guard with twenty-eight years on the job.

But I was writing full time.

I had my share of the glory years of print journalism, thank Jesus. Glicken was given the task of transforming the Women's Section into a features showcase, and he dragooned me to write more adventurous stories.

One day I'd be assigned to cruise into Long Beach from San Diego aboard an aircraft carrier; the next I'd be flying in a Learjet with no more of a hook or an angle other than to write a story about what it's like flying around in a Learjet. He sent four of us out to do a story about Sunday brunch, and we all ended up too drunk to write or even remember what happened.

I walked down to the supply room every week to pick up a handful of Cross pens, a three-hole punch, a few in/out baskets. It was like looting a Staples.

Damn, it was a different time. Only the very weak refrained from cigarettes. There was ceaseless smoking in the newsroom—cigarettes, cigars, pipes—and not so much as a whimper of protest. You don't like it, go stand in front of the building with the other loser nonsmokers. We all but had a fire brigade on retainer to put out trashcan blazes.

Drinking, too, was mandatory. Abstainers ran the risk of getting the nickname of Padre.

Perhaps the most glorious aspect of those days was the bar across the street, shrewdly named the Press Club, by its proprietors, Percy and Otha Ekegren, and presided over by a bartender called Hector the Nectar Director.

The Press Club had newspaper workers in it twenty-four hours a day, despite the fact that it closed at 2 a.m. So, yes, it was closed, but it still had newspaper people in it. You knew you had stayed a bit too long when the printers brought in the next day's paper and you still had a row of upside-down shot glasses (signifying you had a drink coming, compliments of someone-or-other) in front of you. The morning sun beaming through the front-door window was another tip-off.

The Press Club wasn't important as a place to just sit around quaffing loudmouth. It was a Demilitarized Zone, a place where reporters and editors could talk like gentlemen before things descended into fuck-you's being hurled back and forth, all with no consequence whatsoever. The next morning at the plant, things would be back to normal, with absolutely no hard or hurt feelings.

It was where every one of us groused bitterly about not being accorded the proper respect by our editors despite the undeniable evidence of our towering talents and skills.

It was a sacred ground for reporters, pressmen, compositors, ad salesmen, mailers, and editors. Owner Percy was a one-man clearinghouse for information, frequently knowing who was being fired or hired before the principals themselves. At the bar's booths, rumors were launched, deals were struck, careers were made (or torpedoed), contracts were negotiated, and alliances were formed.

One dismal early morning after closing time in 1987, an arsonist burned the Press Club down. Our friend John Beshears, an artist for the paper, stood across Pine Avenue weeping and swearing. Our friend Dave, who wasn't a journalist but worked down the street and was a Press Club regular, stood nearby.

"What are we going to do now?" he asked me. It wasn't a practical question. It was a question delivered with desperation and despondency. It had no satisfactory answer. What were we going to do? It turned out to be nothing.

It wasn't Percy who burned the place down. He didn't even have fire insurance. He and Otha walked away from the business. Nearly three decades later, it's still a vacant lot.

A bunch of us rented a floor in an abandoned secretary college down the street and tried to make that the hangout, but it never stuck; only a handful of reporters swung by, rather than the entire mix of everyone involved in the daily miracle of putting out a newspaper.

It was a Kennedy-assassination equivalent for the *Press-Telegram*. We all died a little bit, and it was the first downward step from the pinnacle of newspapering in Long Beach.

CHAPTER SIX

A Brief, Pre-columnist's Resume

Throughout the years I added to my resumé without leaving my desk. I was a features writer in the early 1980s, when the paper had a features department of forty-two people (including your fashion writer, your food editor, your society columnist, and various arts critics. I was book editor for a few years, rock critic for a few years, TV critic for a couple of years, and copy editor for about a year). I had stories in every section of the paper: TV, Book, Sports (I was pressed into service during the 1984 Olympics to cover the men's 110 high-hurdles; that was pretty weird), Religion, Travel, Food . . .

At various times, I wrote about everything that moved or stood still. Thousands of stories. Don't ask me to remember them all. I covered the national farm crisis in Iowa, interviewed family-killer Dr. Jeffrey

MacDonald in prison in Texas and Arizona, was sent to Hawaii to find out what is was like living on $5 a day (difficult, though the opulent $10 per diem route was easy), interviewing people I enjoyed talking with: David Attenborough, Stephen King, P. J. O'Rourke, John Gregory Dunne and his wife, Joan Didion, Fleetwood Mac's Lindsey Buckingham and Christine McVie. Watched the All-Star game with Dodger catcher Steve Yeager at the Brown Derby. Had breakfast with "Raging Bull" boxer Jake LaMotta at the Polo Lounge the week the film was released. I wrote a daily column from the 1984 Summer Olympics in Los Angeles, spent the last several months with a man dying of cancer while he was trying to prepare his wife and small children for life without him, spent a month living with firefighters, was a clown for one night with the circus, chased kidnappers in Mexico, and trudged up the mountains of Colorado looking for elk.

But, really, I just wanted to write a column. Not for any reason more noble than the fact that my life fascinates me. And it would be selfish to not share it with as many readers as I could reach.

CHAPTER SEVEN

When I Became Us

I snuck in through the back door to the columnist's lofty office. No editor ever had any intention of making me a columnist. Harold Glicken had come up with an idea for a weekly column called What's Hot!, which would be un-bylined and rotated among the staff members.

At that time, I had become enamored of the pronoun "we." E. B. White had used it to nice effect in his little literary musings in the *New Yorker.* (I learned too late that it had been forced upon him and that he despised it.) And, anyway, it fit, since it was to be written by "us," the features writers.

I kicked it off (and right here in the midst of typing this sentence, I took a four-hour break to look for the first one; I failed. Now it belongs to the ages.), putting a bit of humor and personality into what was essentially expected to be a listing of things coming up during the week.

No one wanted to write the second one, so, with a mock-weary sigh ("Nothing gets done around here unless I do it"), I wrote the second, third, and fourth. I'm still counting—and still stuck with the dreadful name "What's Hot!"

"What's Hot!" My dog died.

"What's Hot!" Here's a story we wrote about a guy who played Santa at Christmas that was so unflattering his family believes I caused his eventual death.

I've tried to shake it, but it won't let loose.

Nor will the pronoun. I've tried to abandon it a time or two. But readers, averse to change of any kind (try moving the crossword puzzle's location in the paper if you want to see a reenactment of the villagers in *Frankenstein*.) demanded its return. Turned out they didn't care for "me" as much as "us."

Slowly, the column moved from one day a week to Saturday and Sunday. Then three days a week, which is a typical workload for most "daily" columnists.

By then I had acquired a new editor who liked neither my column nor me. She had turned our pleasant little life into her brand of hell. On the Long Beach City College newspaper, I had thrown a massive Underwood typewriter at an editor. That sort of behavior had since fallen from favor, so my choices now were limited. Rather than taking the easy way out, which would've been to have the offending editor fired and thrown out into the street, I told the assistant managing editor, Carolyn Ruszkiewicz, that I was quitting my job.

"Why don't you just leave features and come work on the City Desk?" she said.

"OK," I said.

"It would be a different kind of column. You'd be writing about things people need to know about: postage rates going up, tax deadlines, street closures, tree trimming," she said.

Sounded like a blast. I already knew from experience that I could easily make the subject of the price of stamps into an essay about the time I played volleyball with a dolphin.

"OK," I said again.

"Maybe three columns a week?"

"Make it five," I said.

She was stunned. She told me years later that she was impressed that I had asked for more work, when everyone else tried to get away with doing less.

I was happy she was impressed, but the truth is I wanted to write five columns because writing three would have given editors two days to monkey around with me by sending me out to do horrifying stories.

Let me share an example of a horrifying story with you:

One spring day in 1980, Harold Glicken told me he wanted me to go around to shoe stores and talk to little kids and their mothers about buying new dress shoes for Easter.

It was the most horrifying thing I could think of. Ideally, you might blunder into a funny quote from a little kid, but it's extraordinarily rare and not worth the brutal experience of walking up to a mother and explaining exactly what it is you have in mind.

Look, I know you think it's not that bad, but it is. Talking to kids is like our own little Vietnam.

"No way," I told Harold.

"Come on, it'll be cute."

"Nope."

"You're doing it."

"Goddammit!" I yelled and stormed out of his office.

A few minutes later, calmed down a bit, I sauntered back in. Let's talk about this calmly like gentlemen.

"Look, I really don't want to do the story. Have someone else do it."

He exploded and started swearing at me, and I exploded and started swearing back, and it finally came down to doing the story or getting fired.

So, the day comes for me to do the story, and I go to work with a stomachache.

I try eating this and drinking that. Smoke a couple of cigarettes. Nothing works, and I can barely stand. I'm cursing myself because if I hadn't argued about the story and had just accepted it; maybe said, "Wow, great idea! It'll be *cute!*" If I had just done that, I could just tell Harold I'm sick and go home.

But now I'm trapped. Barely able to stand and being sent out to go converse with toddlers. The pain gets worse. Intolerable. I have to go in and tell Harold I have a tummy ache.

He doesn't look up from the story he's editing. Rage pools around his shoes. "Just go," he says, simmering with disgust.

I didn't go home. I went to a clinic down the street, then I was rushed to the hospital for an emergency appendectomy. I had waited so long with the pain that my appendix had burst, and a few days after the operation, I developed peritonitis. My temperature hit 104. I wished for blissful death. Eventually, obviously, I recovered.

For all that, it was totally worth it, and I would go through it again to get out of doing a story on Easter shoes.

And that's why I volunteered to write a column five days a week.

CHAPTER EIGHT

The Rock Stars of Journalism

Why is being a columnist the most glamorous and powerful job in the world? You need look no further than the *Dictionary of Occupational Titles* to hear the siren's song of columnist. Read this and you will realize what a hollow life it is that's suffered by every non-columnist:

> "Gathers information and develops subject perspective through research, interview, experience, and attendance at functions, such as political conventions, news meetings, sports events, and social activities. Analyzes and interprets information to formulate and outline story idea. Selects material most pertinent to presentation, organizes material into acceptable media form and format, and writes column or commentary."

Author Don McNay, in the article "Newspaper Columnists as Heroes," termed columnists as "the rock stars of journalism."

Speaking strictly as an egotist, that's why I'm a columnist. But that's not the reason I set my sights on becoming a columnist at a fairly young age. I was playing guitar years before I wrote my first news story in college. If I'd wanted to be a rock star of something, I would have chosen to be a rock star of rock.

And yet I have to cop to some big-headedness. George Orwell, in his essay "Why I Write," lists four driving motives for becoming a writer, and "sheer egoism" tops his list.

No. 2 is "aesthetic enthusiasm," simply enjoying the music of words and the craft of writing. "The firmness of good prose or the rhythm of a good story." In journalism, no one has more freedom to fiddle with the language than a columnist. I've had plenty of late-night phone calls from copy editors so curious about some of my phrasings and phrases: "What do you mean in this sentence: 'The next morning, he fished through the barstow in his jacket pocket, finding a few soggy dollars and a matchbook with a six-digit phone number scrawled on it.'?" *Barstow,* I had to patiently explain, is the wadded up odds and ends that find their way into your pocket in the course of a night at a tavern. Yes, I made that word up, but only because there wasn't a better one at hand.

Next on Orwell's reasons for writing is "historical

impulse," to "find out true facts and store them up for the use of posterity." This isn't, strictly speaking, a driving force in my urge to write, especially as a columnist. "Posterity?" Maybe. Maybe. I mean, who doesn't want their life to drag on for another generation or two after their passing? It makes you feel OK with death, sort of. On the very probable (though not necessarily definite) event of my death, I hope to take some solace in imagining that my passing might spur a spike in sales of this seminal book, with the suddenly ironic, or macabre anyhow, title of *I'm Dyin' Here.*

As for finding and storing facts, I don't really do that. I'm less Orwellian in this aspect and tend more toward the philosophy of the humor columnist Dave Barry, who wrote, "Don't you wish you had a job like mine? All you have to do is think up a certain number of words! Plus, you can repeat words! And they don't even have to be true!"

Finally, Orwell cites "political purpose"—the "desire to push the world in a certain direction." I write about politics occasionally and with great enthusiasm, although I wouldn't claim it as a motivation to write a column. I'm not so inflated in my ego as to think I can push my block, never mind the world, in a certain direction. For me it's a bigger, patio-sized umbrella with which you can have a bit of an effect on a few people. But if you want to make people happy, you probably know not to deal with politics. The only thing you'll get out of it is hate mail and because I am, perversely, a big fan of hate mail, politics is the way to go sometimes. Although you can also irritate plenty of people by writing about animals and yourself.

"The 'irrepressible' Tim Grobaty is a shame to 'journalism.' Snide, immature, irreverent, a slob in looks and manners, 'cutesy' in the use of the English and popish 'We.' I would find it hard to be civil to such a person as he."

"I've been thinking about giving up this liberal, one-sided paper, and I've finally decided, because of you, to do it today."

"You have lost a fan of many years. If you wanted to write opinions, you should have taken the time to learn not to be so offensive."

"I hope they fire you and bring a writer who knows what he is writing about."

"You look like a slob. Who dresses you? Lady Gaga?"

"Why don't you retire already? All you do is write about yourself. That isn't journalism."

"I think it's time for you to retire. We don't care what you do about your dogs or beavers or whatever it is. You write

like you're writing for a high school newspaper. Retire already."

"Why don't you go back to Gilligan's Island and just stay there? That way we won't have to read you. Just go on that one-day—or is it one-hour?—cruise and stay there. Or maybe you should drink more. That way you'd come up with better columns."

"Oh, look! The PT's pompous asshole tries his hand at the usual bullshit. It's good that there are enough twits who swallow his tripe to keep him employed at LB's favorite fish wrapper, because his literary skills and vast ignorance certainly are not."

CHAPTER NINE

"Fine. Die Here."

There are introverted columnists, and there are extroverted columnists. I suppose there are also gradations. While firmly in the introvert camp, I will make the occasional foray into the public eye. I've given a few talks, done some readings, and made some otherwise public appearances, but for me, these take a tremendous amount of courage and an equal amount of Xanax (prescribed by my sainted doctor) and an array of similar fortifications.

Of course, to be a columnist, you have to make the odd appearance, but mostly, you get to hole up in your handsomely appointed suite of offices typing up your thoughts, opinions, and outrages. It's similar to blogging, I suppose, but with a more serious title, an immovable deadline, and at least a modicum of credibility. And that's weird, because bloggers are a big part of the reason why I'm dying here.

Introversion isn't the ideal crippling disease for a columnist. My predecessor and, later, co-columnist Tom Hennessy was way more comfortable doing public appearances. He'd grab a microphone like it was trying to kill his sister. As a result, he was probably the most popular columnist in the *Press-Telegram*'s history, your basic Man of the People, while I lurked in my cubicle and ventured only seldom into roomsful of people. My chronic shyness, further, tends to come across as a sullen hybrid of arrogance and rudeness.

David Foster Wallace said in an interview that shyness and arrogance may go hand in hand. "I think being shy basically means being self-absorbed to the extent that it makes it difficult to be around other people," he confessed to *Rolling Stone* reporter David Lipsky in 1996.

Strangers who approach me in supermarkets and restaurants, I fear, sometimes leave with a measure of dissatisfaction.

My friend Wendy, with whom I have coffee frequently, has witnessed this several times. She always graciously thanks the people who come over, while I either look at my hands or dive under the table in search of a dropped napkin that's not there.

I have a feeling this is a part of my sparkling personality that also has something to do with not straying far from my home.

I've lived all over town—if Long Beach is the world, then I am well traveled. I've lived in six Long Beach council districts, lived in most of its ZIP codes, probably driven or walked or cycled down 90 percent of its streets.

Outside of Long Beach, though, there be dragons. The city's borders are impenetrable. I can't tell you much of anything about the cities that share Long Beach's boundaries.

What does all of this mean for your columnist?

There are several kinds of newspaper columnists (they're like regular humans in that regard)—and I'm limiting myself to those who write for the city pages, because beyond those there are, of course, sports columnists, but also columnists who deal exclusively with health or gardening or fishing or films or books or society. You've got those who dig around uncovering corruption at every level and who birddog city politics. You've got those who insist that every person has a story. (They don't. Toddlers trying on Easter shoes don't have a story.) There are columnists who look for humor everywhere and just type their pieces out at their desk; the worst of them giggle a bit while they do it. That's close to what I do, that last one. Not that I don't hazard the occasional trip outdoors.

Once, for instance, I walked to work.

AN ADVENTURE AFOOT

"Don't go where the hookers go," our wife said to us as we began packing for a cross-city trek.

We were up early—5:30 Monday morning—to make the journey on foot from our house to our office in a fact-finding expedition to determine just how walkable Long Beach is.

A more (or less) pedestrian person would have just taken the word of walkscore.com, a website that has surveyed the country to pinpoint the most walkable cities and neighborhoods.

Walkscore has Long Beach at No. 8, behind such major burgs as San Francisco, New York, Boston, Chicago, and Seattle, and ahead of places you'd think would beat us, including Los Angeles, Portland, Denver, and San Diego.

Walkability, for the survey's purposes, includes such things as density, having a "discernible center" (shopping district, central plaza, main street), parks, nearby schools, and workplaces and several other factors.

All very interesting and perhaps useful, but we just wanted to see if we could survive the trip.

We'd used alternative, non-car travel to traverse the town before. We rode our bike crosstown once, and we thought we were Lewis or Clark. We took a bus, and to hear our account of that trip, you'd have thought we'd discovered a new spice route.

Now we were preparing to do what, as far as we could tell, no man had ever undertaken before: walk

8.4 miles from our home in the Far Eastern territory of the Plaza, up the Los Coyotes Diagonal to the Anaheim Street Corridor to Alamitos to the sparkling, shimmering sea and our cubicle.

We aimed to travel light: a small digital camera, a cell phone, a fresh shirt, ChapStick, our entry card to the office, a notebook, pens, a brush, traveler's checks, Zagat Guide, maps, beads, candy, pocket combs, and bits of shiny glass and bolts of colorful fabric for the peoples in the faraway lands through which we would travel.

Google's latest bit of ingenuity and helpfulness is its new walking directions feature, still in beta, but who among us isn't? It shortened our trip by about a half-mile over what its driving directions had plotted out for us. Armed with the directions, we set out on the expedition.

Walkscore breaks down cities into neighborhoods, and the Plaza had earned a dreadfully mediocre 53 walkability score—only North Long Beach, with a 44, was lower—unless you count Wilmington, with which Walkscore saddled Long Beach, and its score of 29.

We found the Plaza extremely strollable—well beyond its weak score—as we sashayed down past Cubberley School to Metz Street, then to Los Coyotes Diagonal, where we stopped at a mini-mart to dole out some shiny coins with the natives in exchange for water and Gatorade.

From there, we melded seamlessly through Los Altos and the Circle Area (scores of 71 and 76, respectively).

We spent about an hour on the Diagonal, still feeling as spry as a cat before we took the fifteen-minute stroll down Ximeno to Anaheim Street, which, in our youth anyway, was the place where the hookers go.

On Anaheim, a bit east of Temple, we kicked at an empty box of Trojans at a bus stop (we'll read a book at a bus stop; apparently other people have other ways to kill the enemy that is time), a song writing itself in our mind:

"Don't go down where the hookers go, laddy.
"Don't go down were the hookers go, my boy.
"Don't talk to strangers in their cars.
"Don't sit unattended in bars.
"Don't go down where the hookers go, my son."

Our Google Maps Walking Directions printout warned: "Use caution when walking in unfamiliar areas."

The Anaheim Corridor is mostly on the East Side, a neighborhood that scored a rocket-high 81 in Walkscore points—tied with Bixby Knolls—though it didn't give us the same cozy feeling we had in the Plaza.

It wasn't terribly dangerous. One fellow walked around muttering darkly to himself while following us around like a puppy, except maybe differently, for a while until he lost interest.

If you live along the Corridor, there's no compelling reason to have a car—everything's right there: an array of restaurants, bodegas, and such specialty shops as places that sell bottled water and nothing else.

We thought we'd find a lot of stuff on the trip, but

we didn't come across enough to allow us to quit our job: a couple of pairs of brand-new children's shoes with the price tags still affixed, a nice set of some sort of medical pliers that someone had misused as a roach clip, a spray paint can (empty), and the remains of a hobo's brunch—a sample-size bottle of Grey Goose (empty) and a rotten orange.

At Alamitos we could smell the ocean, such as it is. And it was here, at around Sixth Street, by St. Anthony's, the patron saint of missing persons and lost causes, that our body began to eat itself.

Our feet, which had been merrily flopping along, began to holler a bit, our left ankle started sending hot tar up our spine, and our left knee was demanding an immediate transplant.

But the end was in sight: Our office stood like a shining monument down the street, just one full mile (and 43 feet, according to Google), or 22 minutes away.

We stopped and drank a bottle of SmartWater (the energy formula) and sauntered down Ocean in the downtown neighborhood, which, with a score of 87 (thanks to, among other things, the mixed usage of its buildings, the main-streetedness of Pine Avenue and its perhaps accidental pedestrian-centric design, is the most walkable area in Long Beach, comfortably ahead of Belmont Shore and Belmont Heights, with their respective scores of 83 and 82).

It was 9 o'clock—a brisk little three-hour stroll got us to work at the assigned hour. In a minute, we're going to call our wife for a ride home.

OK, so that wasn't as intrepid as a Vasco da Gama expedition. The odds of us getting killed on the journey were minimal, especially in hours past dawn when most of your killers are still asleep. A few years later, we upped the hazard potential by spending the night at a motel along a stretch of Pacific Coast Highway that, as police have told us both before and after we did it, is "a good place to get killed."

MOTEL HELL

We have these whimsical impulses sometimes that we really shouldn't pursue because there's no upside to them other than satisfying our curiosity, while the downside is mayhem and death.

For years we've driven past the Monterey Motel on Cherry Avenue at Pacific Coast Highway and wondered what it would be like to spend the night there, drifting off to sleep with the merry sounds of the street—the choir of prostitutes, gangbangers, drug addicts, and cops chorusing happily outside our window with its cracked glass and shredded screen.

There are worse places in town, we were told. Why settle for the Monterey when we could go to the place where a cop reporter we know met a prostitute who showed her a scar from where a john had cut off a hunk of her flesh and cooked it on a hot plate while she was tied up?

Yes, that would be preferable by far, as long as it had cable.

And more advice poured in. You're not going to enjoy a weird night at a seedy and dangerous motel unless you go to the most northerly part of town, we were told. A waiter suggested "this creepy place near Alamitos on Seventh Street." An old friend told us to go to the place "where the Foothill's 'Baby Duck' died with a strumpet while he was all hopped up on go-fast."

In the end we went with the advice of a Long Beach cop who suggested one of the following: the State Motel, the Poolside Inn Motel, the Tower Motel, or the El Capitan, all on West Pacific Coast Highway near Magnolia and Daisy avenues.

We reached the string of Westside motels at 6 p.m. We didn't want something so luxurious as a pool, so we skipped the Poolside; we missed the turn for the Tower Motel and made a left into the lot at El Capitan. Which, as it turned out, has a pool.

We shoved a wad of twenties ($75 for two beds; $55 for one) at Maria, who manages the motor inn with her husband, Dave.

"You want a TV?" asked Maria. "Most of them only get one or two channels. Four if you're lucky." Dave dragged a cart out, threw an old Zenith set on it, and hauled it off to our room.

"What time's the pool closed?" we asked.

"It's condemned," said Dave. "There are cracks in the gunite and the water keeps leaking out. The owner just keeps it to lure in customers."

We asked him as delicately as we could if his establishment was a good place to run into some trouble, such as getting killed.

"You should go to the Tower for that," he told us. "People over there get scared, and they come over here. We keep a good eye on the place."

The good eye came into play an hour or two later when Dave gave a tenant the heave-ho.

"We have three rules here," Dave told us. "No refunds, no illegal activities and no guests." Unless you cough up $20 for a guest. The ousted tenant had broken rule No. 3 and trudged off carrying his belongings in a plastic garbage bag, toward the Tower.

Dave also has an unwritten Rule No. 4. He doesn't much cotton to transvestites.

Because they decorate the rooms.

"I don't care what they do with their personal life," he said. "But they come in here and move all the furniture around and paint the walls. Sometimes they paint big murals on the walls."

The rooms at El Capitan aren't disastrous. We've stayed in worse places. The walls are painted in festive marigold with Spanish motif trim. You get a chair, a fairly battered dresser, and what we'd like to call an escritoire, but in El Capitan, it's a little table with a drawer.

The air conditioner worked, though someone had busted off the control knob, so you got what you got. Just like outdoors.

There had been two art prints on the wall, but one of the works had been pried off by someone who either overly loved or overly hated it.

We only saw two cockroaches. Didn't check for bedbugs. Most of your motel experts will advise you to not climb under the covers.

At dusk we walked down the highway to an always-busy Eddie's Jr. liquor store built almost entirely out of bulletproof glass, purchased a six-pack of Bud Light and on the way back ran into a guy named Al who was one of our neighbors at the motel.

He invited us into his room where we met his girl-friend, Debbie, who was staying at the motel by the week.

Dave heard about our thirst for peril.

"Oh, man, you should go to the area around Fourth and Orange. We moved here to get away from that place."

A few blocks west of our motel was a little beer bar, the Pit Stop, where Christine was bartending.

We watched the Dodgers win in the bottom of the ninth inning and told Christine we were looking to get our head handed to us.

"You should try the Poolside," she said. She has lived at both the Poolside and the El Capitan at various down points of her life, though now she's got her own place and has jettisoned her ex-boyfriend.

On the bar's back wall was a sign, "Happy Birthday, Bernard!" We asked if Bernard had enjoyed his party.

"He didn't show up," she said. "Thank God. He's my ex."

We checked out some of the other hotels on the stretch of PCH.

They were all as quiet as El Capitan. We walked onto the court at the Poolside Motel, with its sign redundantly touting "Heated Pool," though it looked like someone had tried to block out the "Heated" part.

It wasn't a big place, but we couldn't find the pool.

"We got rid of it about six years ago," the night manager told us.

Back at El Capitan we sat in a plastic chair for a few hours, watching the passing groups of youngsters, old guys, your regular old street people. A little after midnight, a guy with eyes as big as pocket watches walked off the street and asked us if we had anything.

"Some things," we said. "What are you after?"

"Speed," he said.

"Nope, don't have any speed."

"It's cool. I got a place lined up, just thought I could maybe save myself a walk."

We watched him bound off and then went in and hit the hay.

In terms of getting beat up, robbed, shot, knifed, propositioned, or even worried, the evening was a bleak failure. But we learned a lot in a part of town we'd never much explored, especially the part about the transvestites.

Right, so I go out from time to time, but am I dodging the big question? Yes, I left my house to walk to work, but it's the same place I've worked for almost forty years. I stayed at a dangerous motel. In the town where I live. Why not do what everyone else seems to do, which is toss the family in the car, rent a U-Haul, and move to another city? Who knows, maybe an editor from another paper has to have me on his staff.

What? You don't know. It could happen.

"You gotta get outta here and move to New York," one great investigative reporter used to tell me over drinks at the Press Club when I was still in my twenties. He had done investigative pieces for the *New York Times*, had been an editor for the old *Saturday Evening Post*, where he worked with such cubs as Joan Didion. He had written a book about Howard Hughes, which had been serialized by *TIME* magazine and made into a television special.

"Leave me alone," I'd keep telling him.

"Fine. Die here," he'd say, making it sound like the last word on the matter.

"No, seriously. Move to New York. Long Beach is no place to wind up. You want to spend your WHOLE LIFE here? I can get you the people to talk to. You could get a job there easily."

"Jim," I'd say, because his name was Jim Phelan. "I don't know what I want to do. I like it here, though."

Phelan had once worked at the *Press-Telegram*, but he couldn't stand it. Too small time.

It was flattering, though, as was the time an editor from the *Charlotte Observer* came to the *Press-Telegram* to critique the work of the staff writers.

"I can't say anything bad about your writing," he told me when it was my turn. "I would hire you in a second."

My wife had just been to Charlotte on business and she loved the town.

We didn't have any children yet; it was just a matter of packing up the truck and moving to the South, where I was anxious to develop a laconic accent and, I don't know, reinvent myself. Maybe wear a hat or something.

I spoke to one of the top editors at work about transferring to the *Observer*. I thought maybe he'd beg me not to. Instead, he gave me a righteous dressing down. "You're lazy, you're a slob, you look like shit, you don't know how to report."

Yeah, well, OK, sure, if you just want to pick away at the flaws.

"I think they want me because I can write humor," I said from deep down in the pit I'd been thrown.

"Big deal. You think a humor columnist can win a Pulitzer?"

The next year Dave Barry won a Pulitzer. But with my editor threatening to tell his Charlotte counterpart, with whom he was friends, the litany of my flaws, I stayed in Long Beach, and, I guess it was probably to my relief.

Years later, another editor, giving me a job evaluation, told me, "You're a great writer, you're a huge help to the paper on a lot of levels. But you're lazy."

"Robbie," I told him. "If I wasn't lazy, I wouldn't be here."

And that, finally, I suppose, is the honest answer to the question of why I have worked at the same place, stayed in the same city.

There's a song by Tom Waits that always strikes my heart. It's about a man who stayed in the same town all his life, though, he rasps, "Sometimes the music from the dance will carry across the plain, and places that I'm dreaming of, do they dream only of me?"

Of course, whatever it was that kept me in Long Beach in my youthful years when I was expected to be more restless and certainly more ambitious has mellowed into something more closely resembling Yeats's easy dream of finding satisfaction with his nine bean rows, or to put a loftier cast on it, the Buddhist's quest for the cessation of hankering.

But probably just laziness.

CHAPTER TEN

"Computers Could Replace Newspapers"

Though I began writing on word processors in the late 1970s, home computers were still a ways off, and the World Wide Web was perhaps a twinkle in some visionary nerd's eye, but personal computers certainly weren't on my radar.

The gizmos seemed like just another novelty. High tech, for sure, and expensive, with limited applications as far as I could tell. They were touted as great ways to file recipes and maintain holiday mailing lists.

I was fairly infatuated by them, especially when they became so sophisticated you could draw geometric shapes with them and then fill in that shape by dragging a "bucket" of "paint" and filling in the shape. Civilization's pinnacle. With my first Apple computer, my wife and I took turns making business cards with gaudy fonts and buckets full of hound's-tooth patterns. We would dream of businesses we could open, and then rush over to the computer to design business cards for them.

Then, after having exhausted the new toy's capabilities, we'd watch a little tube and hit the hay.

Being farsighted, I could see the potential. I could see the day where these things could keep track of the food you have in the house, and maybe all your other stuff. I typed in the make and description of my guitars. I started to type in the titles and artists of all my records, but got tired of it somewhere after the Allman Brothers.

I didn't even sort of dream of what computers would eventually do. I certainly didn't think they would try to kill me and my family by making me obsolete.

SOMEDAY WE'LL ALL BE
USING COMPUTERS ON MARS

In the late 1970s and early 1980s, we were the youngest reporter for these newspapers and therefore the go-to guy for newfangled contraptions like the new generations of telephones (You can talk to two different people at once! You can buy a machine that will take a message!! You can store phone numbers in it for "speed dialing"!!!), and this whole business about "home computers."

In 1981, one of our befuddled editors wanted to know what was the deal with these "computer" things that were starting to pop up at RadioShack and Typewriter City. "Are people going to be putting them in their houses, or what?"

"Yeah, if they're morons with too much money," we replied with cynical savvy.

Just as GPS-based search engines would one day be relentlessly touted as a way to find pizza in any city you find yourself in, salespeople for early home computers praised the machine's capability for sorting and storing. You could put a hundred recipes in one of these $2,000, 64-kilobyte bad boys. No Christmas mailing list was too big. You could play chess with it.

You got the bucks, you could pop for an acoustic coupler that would hook up to computers through your, as we've already seen, futuristical telephone.

If you had the knack for it, you could program your computer to do things for you. Or purchase programs for, as we noted, "almost every conceivable application." They come, we patiently explained in an article to our wide-eyed readership, on either cassettes or on (here's a new word to add to your tech-packed lexicon) "floppy disks," "cards that are coated with magnetic tape."

We introduced two computers to readers that they might be interested in: The mighty, mighty Radio-Shack TRS-80 ($599 with a 12-inch monitor and a RadioShack tape recorder as data-cassette storage) and the Apple II, which was costlier (big surprise) at $2,638 packed with the maximum 48k of RAM.

Our sage opinion at the time was you've gotta be a spectacular cook or have a seasonal mailing list bigger than Santa's to justify the cost.

In a statement that was terribly prescient, the editor of the computer magazine *Interface Age* told us that home computers "smacks a little of '1984' or 'Future Shock.' It tends to take away people's initiative. There are still a few things that people think should remain in their domain."

An information systems expert at Cal State Long Beach seemed pretty plugged in, though he didn't see the breadth of the takeover of computers. "I see the day coming when all homes have computers. Like, there's this guy who has programmed his computer with his house so that it will water his lawns and open and close his windows."

Great. Is that all there is? "Well," said the guy from Cal State, "they could replace newspapers. They could replace libraries. Why buy a book when you could plug right into a system and call up whatever you want to read?"

The *Interface Age* editor noted, "First, technology needs to be accepted by the public. Right now the general public is scared to death of computers."

We went and wrote the story, secure in the knowledge that our job would be essential for years to come.

And whoever read that story, read it in the newspaper.

And, of course, the Internet became accessible with the Web, giving everyone with a computer and a modem the ability to, if you will pardon the popular muddled metaphor, surf the Information Superhighway.

Once again, the Web had limited use. When I managed to tap into it for the first time (when there were no easy browsers like those that would come later), I immediately looked up the lyrics to REM songs. After that, I couldn't think of anything I wanted to know.

You could download text games, such as *Adventureland*, ("You are standing at the end of a road before a small brick building . . . " and you typed commands like "ENTER" or "GO IN") if you could spare the 300k storage it required.

Eventually, the newspaper assigned me to cover the emerging Web in a column called WWWhat's Hot! (As an apologetic aside here, I need to absolve myself: I've never been allowed to name my columns. I'm not sure, at this remove, who to blame for "What's Hot!" or, briefly, "What's Up" or maybe most egregiously, "WWWhat's Hot!")

Knight-Ridder syndicated the column, so my words went out to readers all over the country, appearing in such publications as the *Cedar Rapids Gazette*, the *Lima* (Ohio) *News*, the *Amarillo Daily News*, and the *Panama City News Herald*. There wasn't a newspaper in this country too small to run my columns.

In 1991, I managed to parlay the Web writings into

a brief career as a columnist for *Variety.* The Holly-wood publication carried the column until the first calamitous collapse of Silicon Valley, but it was fun while it lasted. Our assignment was to find Web applications for Hollywood.

IT TAKES A MOGUL

Day 1: I decide to make a movie.

Day 2: Depression sets in. This is going to be more difficult than I had anticipated. I hadn't even thought about things like, well, I don't have a camera, for instance. No camera, no stars, no screenplay, no ideas. The closest thing to perfection in my life is my ignorance of moviemaking.

Day 3: I recall that the entire corpus of human knowl-edge, including How to Make a Movie, is on the Web. I consult the all-knowing Webucational site SoYou Wanna.com, which is packed with instructions to teach you just about anything, including how to get a ferret, how to speak with an Irish accent, and how to convert to Buddhism—and "SoYouWanna Make a Low-Budget Movie."

Who said anything about low budget? I actually wanted to make a $140-million movie, but apparently that would entail going to a real college and arranging meetings with moguls. I wanted to get this thing wrapped up in a couple of weeks so I could move on to something else, like buying a ferret.

Day 4: Big, big day. Following the SoYouWanna advice, I nailed down a script, cast, camera, and a couple cans of film. A monkey could put out a movie.

There are plenty of screenwriters, generally of the fledgling variety, who stick their scripts on the Internet in hopes of landing a deal. I spent the better part of several minutes scrolling through scores of offerings on The Hollywood Script Readers' Digest and checked out pitches for such projects as *Maternity Leave* (*Meet the Parents* meets *After Hours*), *Kidbomb* (*Independence Day* meets *Freaky Friday*) and *The Copy Machine* (the humor of *There's Something About Mary* enters the supernatural world of *The Sixth Sense*) before I settled on the rare non-hybrid film, *Oui Are Family,* which was cyberpitched by its author Franco McLavery, as *The Mob Goes Light in the Loafers.*

In search of talent, I discovered there's no shortage of work-seeking actors online. I took a chance on the World Wide Stars site, and it paid off handsomely. There's a tough wiseguy-lookin' Chip Nuzzo, who played a gangster in the movie *Gun Crazy* and who speaks Italian. Then, perhaps as a sidekick, there's Rick Casale, who's done such thuggish turns as Louie in *DragonStreet* and Vito Rizzo in *Passport: Vendetta* and who can—and I've gotta have my writer work this in—handle animals and juggle. The screenplay called for a gay Frenchman and on the website I decided on Henri Boyer, who speaks French and trained at the Conservatoire National Supérieur d'Art

Dramatique in Paris, to make the stretch in this demanding role.

While still back in my earlier hours of learning how to make a movie, I'd had the good fortune to blunder into a site bearing a similar name to SoYouWanna .com. It was called Ya Wanna Make a Movie? and it led me to a site full of used film gear, including the rough-and-tumble 16mm Arriflex Model M-B Camera. This bad boy comes coupled to an Angenieux Paris F:9, 5-57mm 1:1.4-2.2 zoom lens. No idea what that means.

Also, at the same site, I "stole" about 800 feet of film stock for just $150.

I can smell—figuratively speaking—Oscar.

Day 5: Logistics, logistics, logistics. Happily, I live in a town that's terribly film friendly. They're all the time blowing things up here for the movies, including several cars and a service station for scenes in the *Lethal Weapon* series. I swing by the website Long Beach Locations and check out several properties represented by longtime location scout John Robinson, who assures me he can get me a really cool restaurant, with a billiards room and a cigar room for, oh, let's call it $7,500 a night if I shoot afterhours. He'll put me in a big mansion on Country Club Drive for around the same price, and the oldest gay bar in town for a little less.

My dog-eared printout of SoYouWanna Make a Low-Budget Movie advises me to barter with points against future profits in lieu of cash. So far I've got that points-against-gross pie sliced to little wedges so thin you can read through them, so by the time I get down to craft services, I'm pretty well tapped out. There are hundreds of places that will feed my cast and crew and nearly all have goofy names. I pass on Josh'es Nosh, the Movable Feast, and A Touch of Craft and settle on the decidedly affordable Franks A Lot out of lovely Bell Gardens.

Day 6: Depression returns. All I've got is a goofy script, a bunch of actors no one's heard of, a camera I can't figure out how to use (and film that's the wrong size), and my refrigerator's packed with Tupperware containers full of wieners. I fill my days now training my ferret, Randy, with my faithful printout of SoYouWanna Get a Ferret at hand. Check out Step. No. 2 in "Litter box Training": Whenever he does the "ferret-potty dance" (spinning around and backing his rear into a corner), put him in the litter pan.

That make you queasy? Not me. I've been in the movie business, boys, toss me the ferret.

So the Internet had arrived, and what a pleasure and a boon it was. Prior to search engines, like Yahoo! and whatever was on AOL, reporters could throw out mountains of reference books. No more treks down the hall to look up Teddy Roosevelt's cabinet members in the encyclopedia (and Teddy Roosevelt was testing the limits of the sadly out-of-date set of Americanas; you wanted to know anything after the

Louisiana Purchase, you'd have to run down to the public library).

Librarians in particular, and editors, too, and college professors and other teachers warned that most of what people found on the Web was bogus—they had their own jobs to save—but on my trips to the library, I found librarians pounding away at Yahoo! to answer callers' questions.

Now, suddenly you could look up almost everything you needed to know. You could find out who was the vice president of a company without having to go through a lengthy discussion with the company's PR department. It made journalism a lot easier.

Maybe a few of us blundered into prescience by crowing, "This changes everything!"

CHAPTER ELEVEN

The Leaving

One day around this time, a reporter left, as one will, and his vacancy wasn't filled. Can you believe it? The grousing was deafening. How are we supposed to cover the news without whatever beat that guy had? Then another took a job elsewhere, another retired. By the late 1980s, the paper was ten reporters shy of a full newsroom. The paper was shrinking by attrition. Money was tight. Suddenly editors were looking for quarters in the long-abandoned ashtrays. Nobody was going anywhere on a fancy airplane.

Buyouts were offered and buyouts were taken. I lost best friend after best friend; people I had worked and laughed and drank with for twenty years. At just one goodbye "party" in the winter of 1995, I found myself sadder than I am at most funerals. My long-time friend John Beshears, with whom I had driven back from Mexico, Missouri, with whatever possessions he had decided to keep following his mother's death—he was leaving. Dan Winkel, with whom I had written screenplays and who was the godfather of my daughter—he was leaving. People with whom I had vacationed often, renting large cabins in the mountains, gone houseboating with on Lake Powell, sprawled on beaches in Maui and Kauai, taken road trips up the coast. They were leaving, taking the money and hoping for work elsewhere. I have lost touch with all of them.

In 1997, when the *Press-Telegram* began losing money like it was its new, enthusiastic hobby. The paper, including its 108 full-time employees was sold to Dean Singleton. We humans were thrown in as part of the deal, along with the building, presses, staplers, and pica poles.

It was what passed for a bloodbath in a peaceful pressroom. Hat in hand, each employee had to reapply for a job. I showed up for the interview wearing what I usually wear: jeans, T-shirt, unbuttoned long-sleeve shirt.

It wasn't a grueling interview.

"You live in Long Beach?" asked Singleton.

"Yes. All my life."

"You like your job?"

"I love my job. My last job was teaching algebra to junior high-school students. I don't know any algebra. I don't think they'd want me back."

He sort of laughed.

Later, a senior editor called me up to tell me I was rehired! Turned out my writing style was remarkably similar to the columnist they let go last week. More remarkably, I got to keep my salary, while many others had their pay slashed by 25 percent or were laid off (that is to say, not rehired).

So I went back to work in my new job as my own replacement. Big shoes to fill.

CHAPTER TWELVE

Nothing, and Other Great Ideas

Every day another column, another idea needed. Five days a week, fifty-two weeks a year, ten years a decade, ten decades a century, ten centuries a millennium, ten millennia an eon. It gets intergalactic after a while. It can start to gang up on you.

A responsible and mature columnist will write ahead, keeping a couple-three columns in the can against the day when writer's block or a gaping nothingness offers no compelling thoughts or ideas.

My irresponsibility is matched only by my immaturity. Only rarely does the day greet me with an idea for the next day's column. It makes for a scary morning sometimes.

Every couple of months I get a request from a college or high school journalism student who has been assigned to "shadow" a reporter for a day. I've always had to offer my regrets. On a typical day, shadowing me would go, almost invariably, like this:

7 a.m.: The student watches me sitting in my hot tub at home as I try to think of an idea for the day's column. I can't think of anything. I blame it on the student for distracting me, though, truthfully, I've never had a good idea while sitting in the hot tub.

7:30 a.m.: I make the student take my dogs for a walk and rustle up some flapjacks while I take a shower and get all dolled up for work.

8:30 a.m.: The student watches me check out Facebook and read my e-mails. Here's one from a publicist asking to try out a new kind of sandal: "The super soft Lycra strap caresses feet without risk of abrasion and is fully adjustable for a smooth fit, while antimicrobial treatment protects against sweaty socks and the unpleasant smells often accompanying a post-workout or playing sports." There are twenty similar pitches.

9 a.m.: We go to Starbucks. I get a turkey and Havarti sandwich for later and a venti cappuccino for the drive. The student gets a tall, upside-down, half-skinny half-1 percent extra hot split quad shot (two shots decaf, two shots regular) latte with whip.

9:30 a.m.: Turn on the computer and look at it for a while. Student is quiet. A little too quiet. I introduce the student to our public editor Rich Archbold, who performs a few dozen duties in his role. Talking to strangers is his favorite duty. He'll start with chattering about his days in Omaha in the 1950s. By the time he gets to 1978, we'll be home in bed. The student will wind up writing a paper on Archbold.

There are a number of things that can happen at this point, but they all involve an idea. I come in with a blank slate, and I wait for, well, just about anything.

1. An earthquake would be nice. Working in Southern California, an earthquake has pulled my fat out of the fire on more than one occasion.

SHAKEN, BUT NOT STIRRED

It's funny how one strives to maintain one's dignity, even with the absolute certainty of horrid death lurking just moments away.

We sat at our desk on the 14th floor of the Arco Center a bit before noon on Tuesday, and did we mention that the building was whipping around like a water wiggle—a water wiggle full of people who should have been slobbering in terror and screaming for their lives?

And, while our body was shaking us by our lapels and shouting, "SCREAM! Why are you just sitting there? It's an earthquake! Your life is ending NOW! SCREAM!" we managed to keep a more or less straight face while remaining anchored professionally at our desk in our chair—a chair that we were pretty sure would soon be rocketing through the ether, high over the port.

Our next-door-cubicle occupant, police reporter Tracy Manzer, hardened beyond reason and pleasure by a life of crime, was playing a word-search puzzle on Facebook like some kind of old lady with a lot of cats, when the quake hit, and throughout the eternity's duration of the quake, she quietly informed us about how "the building is supposed to whip around violently during an earthquake—and, oh look, I found the word 'what-a-bunch-of-pansies'—so how about everybody stops hollering like tourists and settles down?"

Even though some inner pie-in-the-sky, look-on-the-sunny-side of us was blabbing about how this, too, would pass, a bigger, bawdier part of us was informing us that this was the Big One.

"Remember how you've been going around telling everyone that Southern California was never going to experience another earthquake?" said Mr. Bawdy Side. "Here's the Big One for you. You brought this on yourself. It should serve to demonstrate your stupidity, the serendipity of calamity and the terrible swiftness of death."

Well, don't we feel sheepish now?

We haven't always been this mock-dignified in a quake. We recall a temblor about eighteen years ago, when our offices were only on the second floor, although it was the second floor of a building in disrepair. In that one, we disregarded every bit of advice about staying indoors and instead sprinted down the stairwell to the sweet outdoors, tossing slow-moving old ladies out of our way like they were bags of lawn clippings.

"You've lived your lives," we all but shouted at them. "We have so much more to give!"

Home alone and lots younger during the bigger quakes of Northridge and Sylmar, we dealt with danger by careening around the house switching wildly between prayers and beggings for mercy to a whole host of various deities, with long strings of angry obscenities and swear words thrown in for the secular side.

All of this just shows the wonderful diversity of ways in which we face danger and how we react in emergencies. We don't even know who we are half the time.

But in all instances, there's always the giddiness that comes when safety follows peril. That's what we're feeling now, sitting here giggling like an idiot and happy to be alive and sitting still.

And now that our work here is finished, we'll be hopping into our car and driving into the loving arms of the freeway, where nothing can go wrong.

---

2. You could remember you were supposed to deliver your daughter's Girl Scout Cookies to your fellow employees and go down to your car to fetch them. Maybe that has some sort of column possibility. Something about the seasonal joy attending the release of a new batch of Girl Scout Cookies; the dad's rite of passage in doing all the work. I know, seems pretty weak, but let's go get the cookies.

DO-SI-D'OH, FALSE ALARM

Oh, like you've never made a mistake.

Like you've never helped out your beloved and beautiful daughter by selling Girl Scout Cookies to your coworkers at the office.

Like you've never struggled with a mammoth box full of cartons of Girl Scout Cookies when they finally arrive, hauling them out of your minivan parked three levels below street level and into the busy lobby of the place where you work, which is one of a pair of fifteen-story-high towers that make up the ARCO Center.

Like you've never started to strain beneath the weight of that box of cartons of Girl Scout Cookies, your knees buckling just a bit, a spark of pain beginning to gather at the base of your spine. You don't need us to remind you that you're not the young, strapping man you used to be.

Like you've never, to help ease the burden while you're waiting for an elevator to take you up to the 14th floor, set the box on top of a fire alarm box that jutted out of the wall (and, a few seconds later you will find a quiet spot in your mind amid the riotous tumult going on all around you, in which you will find the opportunity to become miffed that they don't make fire alarm boxes like they used to. Whatever happened, you'll wonder as calmly/curiously as Andy Rooney, to the old fire alarm boxes? The pig-iron ones with the heavy glass that you had to take a flying run at with a hammer or hatchet to bust into to set them off? When did they start making them as touchy and sensitive as Dr. Phil? When did they become so flimsy that they will go off as a result of a little Girl Scout Cookie–related pressure? But, as we've said, this will come a few seconds later).

At first you don't realize the cause and effect of your making use of what you assume to be a manly and ultra-sturdy fire alarm box as a weight-distribution aid and the sudden explosion of activity that comes in the next moment.

Now, strobe lights are flashing and sirens are screaming and a metallic, Big Brothery–sounding voice cackles from speakers placed, as far as you know, all over the world: "Attention! Attention! A FIRE HAS BEEN REPORTED!"

And then the increasingly irritating and sinisterly techno-sounding take-charge voice goes into a looped and intensely urgent riff about the elevators being shut down—"DO NOT TAKE THE ELEVATORS!" which you totally want to do because, swear to god, you've never been this embarrassed in your life—and he/it goes on, robotically spewing all kinds of dire, apocalyptic chatter, which is soon enough accompanied by a parade of irate businessmen and frumpy attorneys and sassy, gum-snapping clerical helpers and panicky plaintiffs from the halls of the labor lawyers (was it your imagination, or did you see leaping deer and panicky wild horses and chattering squirrels at the vanguard of the exodus?) all cascading into the lobby and out the doors to the safety of the rest of the world, directed by orange-jacketed floor captains who have been prepared for just this moment in history—while you stand there with your gigantic box of cartons of Girl Scout Cookies amid the wailing sirens and attention-demanding disembodied voices and one woman is looking at you and hollering, "You set it off! You set it off with that box! You laid that box on the fire alarm and set it off!" and Big Brother, for the twelfth or fourteenth time is getting screechier: "Attention! Attention! A FIRE HAS BEEN REPORTED" and amid that automatic dialogue you're hearing snippets of disgruntlement as the urgency of doom recedes to be replaced by maddening inconvenience: " . . . guy over there . . . big box . . . cookies or something . . . set it off . . . moron . . . don't have enough work to do as it is that I gotta waste my morning doing this all because some idiot . . . "

Or maybe not. Maybe that hasn't happened to you, but it sure happened to us, and we didn't like it. And we still have three more giant boxes of cartons of Girl Scout Cookies to bring in.

Get 'em while they're hot.

---

3. Something interesting occurs right in your front yard. This is the rarest and best of all possibilities for the idea-seeking columnist. You're not even at the part of the day when you've bothered to start thinking yet, when you look out the window and see that your work, save for the typing, is finished for the day.

WE'VE GOT A WAY WITH WATER

We have secret powers.

We're curled up like a cat on the window seat in the living room while our daughter is watching MTV and eating a Pop-Tart before school (Parenting? Oh, we gave up on that a long time ago. Lotta work.), and this guy in a gimme cap and an orange DayGlo vest walks slowly down the middle of our street holding a couple of, say, 18-inch-long welding rods, each bent at one end at 90 degrees to form a handle.

He's holding them pointing ahead like dueling pistols and keeps walking until they sort of spin inward against his chest. He pulls out a can of green DayGlo spray paint from a special spray-paint holster, and makes some marks on our street, then continues along with the welding rods until they move inward again, and he paints again, and he walks again, and we're all "What the???"

We go outside because, again like a cat, we're curious.

We've made up a little task for ourselves, which is to carry a Pop-Tart wrapper across the street to throw it out in a neighbor's trashcan, causing our path to cross the guy with the rods (and to cause some near-future Dumpster-diver to shake his head sadly at the woeful nutritional habits of our neighbor).

"Say," we say, "those wouldn't be divining rods would they?"

He says. "Yeah, they are. I have no idea how they work, but they do."

We're like a kid meeting a superhero. "Do you have secret powers?" we ask, using our special golly-mister voice of awe.

"No, anyone can do it. Would you like to try?"

"Wood Eye!" we practically shout.

He hands over the welding rods. "I'm looking for water mains," he says (we never got his name; it was still breakfast time; we weren't in full Reporter Mode yet). "When I find one, I mark it with the paint, so when they come to dig up your street," (They're digging up our street?) "they won't hit a pipe."

OK, we're thinking. Enough with the technical mumbo-jumbo. Let's go find water, boys!

We hold the divining rods, all new-school-looking compared to the slingshot-shaped branch that dowsers used back in the day. And we slowly march for about 10 yards. Nada, waterwise. We return to our dowser dude, crestfallen.

"Don't hold them so tight," he advises. "Just hold them loose and let them turn when they want."

We walk over what's been marked as a water-main pipe and maybe one of the rods twitches a bit. Maybe we're making it do it, like we used to make a Ouija board spell out our girlfriend's name. We have no control over what our brain wants us to do.

"No, look," says the Water Wizard. "Hold your thumb up like this," and he's adjusting our grip on the welding rods. We walk a bit and YAHHHH! the rods turn in and form a little X in front of us. We have discovered water, or pipes, anyway. We're like some sort of miracle man.

We thank our mentor profusely for the opportunity. Dowsing, divining, whatever. We always thought it was hooey, but it actually works, albeit only in the hands of someone with mystical powers.

Our daughter is waiting for us on the porch when we bounce happily home.

"What were you doing?" she asks.

We explain the whole process, about the rods, and about us having secret powers and everything.

She says, "They're digging up our street?"

---

4. Look around for things on your desk. It always worked for Andy Rooney. Once, I had a birthday card from my sister on my desk. It was an hour before deadline. There wasn't an earthquake in sight.

A CARD, A MONKEY & SWEET MEMORIES

One of our earliest happy memories is that of waiting for the ice-cream man, lying on our back on the front lawn of our great-grandmother's house on Keever Avenue, using a protruding root from a giant sycamore tree as a pillow and watching a monkey swing happily from branch to branch.

Sometimes we don't trust our memory 100 percent, but we've always remembered a monkey in that scene. We're thinking maybe it really was a monkey. One that was kept as a pet somewhere before breaking for horrible freedom. The kid who lived in the house behind our great-grandmother's had a mess of animals in cages. Squirrels, a couple of raccoons. No reason he couldn't have acquired a monkey somewhere along the way, and then that monkey got out and we saw it while waiting for the ice-cream man.

The Good Humor Man, to be precise, because in those days, your mobile ice cream came from a guy all dressed in white, with a flashing smile and a shock of shiny jet-black hair who would, for a nickel or a dime, hand you a Popsicle or a Fudgsicle or a 50-50 bar from his franchised truck.

This particular memory came snapping back at us after our sister finally gave us a birthday card and a couple of gifts on Monday—a month and change after our birthday but, suspiciously, just a day after hers.

The card shows a picture of a kid, looks to be about four, frolicking on the grass in the shade of a giant non-sycamore. Off to the side of the card's cover, we are urged, by poet Kathy Fagan, to recall "how the melody of a single ice cream truck can rise from the streets of your city and bring with it every year you have ever known."

We leave the card's nostalgia for a little more: The gifts were things from our past, as well. A carousel poker-chip holder that belonged to our late father, probably for most of his life. We don't play much poker. We can. Do not ever make the mistake of thinking we cannot play poker. We just don't.

We vaguely recall getting in a bit of trouble once for misusing the poker-chip set. How we misused it is anyone's guess now. These aren't classy poker chips.

You could almost play tiddlywinks with them. No reason to get all excited, Pop. It's not like we let our hair get all long and down our back. That would come later.

Finally, because our sister travels more than Robert E. Lee's horse, she was in Dallas a couple of days ago, and she bought us a box of Lamme's Texas Chewie Pecan Pralines, which doesn't need to mean anything to you, but our mom used to get a box of these for Christmas and hide them. And we would find them, and we would eat them.

We couldn't not do it. They were literally sinfully good. We knew the difference between venial sin and mortal sin, and we sought the candies out and with malice aforethought, took them, one by one, and ate them until they were all gone, which was usually about January 3 following Christmas.

We would get yelled at, punished with chores and restrictions. We'd go to confession, telling Padre that we ate eighteen Texas Chewie Pecan Pralines without permission (We didn't want to say "stole." Such an ugly word.), say a few prayers, and be absolved, once again close to heaven. And we were, as required, repentant and truly sorry. But only after they were all gone.

Now we have a whole, albeit mini, box (at airport prices, an eighteen-pack would cost more than a first-class upgrade), which we can eat without fear of after-life reprisal. They will be gone before we get our sister a birthday present.

So, we put all that stuff away. The pralines out in

the Barn, the poker chips up in the tertiary liquor cabinet (if you see us pour you a drink out of the tertiary cabinet, know that you are not loved by us), and the card by our nightstand.

We hit the hay late, reading a bit of *The Interrogative Mood* by Padgett Powell, a strange and wonderful and hyper-inquisitive book written entirely in the interrogative mood. We arrived quickly at this passage:

"If we heard the ice-cream man right now dinging down the street and we scrambled for some change, maybe even from within the sofa, and went out there breathlessly and caught him, what would you order?"

Right now? At 2-something in the morning? A Push-Up full of rainbow sherbet.

We picked up the card and looked at it again.

The kid, we are meant to suppose, is waiting for the ice-cream man, he is killing time pleasantly enough, swinging his feet up high and looking at his shoes, or, perhaps, looking farther up, into the branches, where a monkey swings down the block, through the bright early spring leaves, from branch to branch to branch.

---

5. **Shadow the shadower.** One of the few questions a student will ask me before I duck out of shadowing is where do my ideas come from. Everyone who has ever asked me a question has asked me how I get ideas for a column. I never knew the answer until I decided to write a column about how I get ideas for a column.

FOR US, A POSSUM IS A GOOD IDEA

We had a colossal brain explosion last week. We think we might've actually died for a second. We certainly died in terms of a public performance.

We were a guest on Charter Communications' *Straight Talk,* hosted by Art Levine and, after a bit of unreliable math, we came to the agreement that we've written something on the order of 4,000 columns in our young life. The inevitable question came next:

"Where do you get all those ideas?"

It wasn't exactly a "gotcha" question. We're asked the question at least once a week. You'd think we would have formulated at least a stock answer for it.

The way this particular question was phrased by Levine, we think, was what made our body shut down.

First, we saw 4,000 column ideas streak across our mind in 2 seconds. In the same time span we thought, in hyperspeed, that the column about a possum crawling on our head in our sleep came from a possum crawling on our head in our sleep, and the column about trying to buy a talking toy parrot at the Reform Party presidential convention in 2000 came from trying to buy a talking toy parrot, and so on, times 4,000, then everything went blank and white, and we started panicking and finally our brain said, "We're losing power! Shut this guy down stat! He's gonna blow!"

It was mortifying. We kept waiting for someone to holler "Cut!" but it never came. Hours passed.

"I see I've left you speechless," said Levine, before tossing us an even softer softball, and our life continued apace.

There are scant and unsatisfactory answers to the question: The ideas just come to us magically; people send them in hastily scrawled letters; they come via e-mail, Facebook, and Twitter; they come from phone calls and conversations; they're adapted from other people's ideas; they're torn from today's headlines; they come to us in the shower. All true, but all just sort of skimming the truth. If we have, in fact, written 4,000 columns, the ideas have come from hundreds of sources, some solid, some ethereal.

After our on-air humiliation, we went to the Internet—a huge source of ideas—to ask it the simple question: "Where do we get our ideas?" The Internet didn't panic or melt down. It did, however, send us to a lot of highfalutin' overthinking by idea-havers.

Then, we found an essay by author Neil Gaiman, who has billions of ideas. Turns out he, too, has had to grapple with the eternal question, and for years, he had no satisfactory answer, until he was asked the question by a seven-year-old girl in his daughter's class on career day.

"And I realized I owed them an answer," wrote Gaiman. "They weren't old enough to know any better. And it's a perfectly reasonable question, if you aren't asked it weekly."

Gaiman told the little girl: "You get ideas from daydreaming. You get ideas from being bored. You get ideas all the time. The only difference between writers and other people is we notice when we're doing it."

Perfect.

He went on and on, as he tends to do in his books, but he needn't have. That's pretty much it. When you have a thought, it flitters away. When we have one, we write 800 words on it. We're not saying we're great at it. If 4,000 is the number of columns we've written, only 3,800 would be what you'd term great, unless you prefer the term "spectacular," or "deathless."

We'll be honest—and this is how ingrained the idea-having process is when you have to do it every day—when we're in the midst of a sizeable earthquake, we don't throw our body over our children to protect them from falling ceilings. We think of what our opening paragraph will be on our quake column.

Even on September 11, 2001, we wondered, as bodies fell from the heavens, what will our angle be on this?

Look, you're asleep one night after midnight and you begin to dream. Someone, you dream, is gently caressing your head, stroking your hair. Your spouse stirs, hearing you go *mmm* contentedly and maybe wonders if you're dreaming of someone else.

The caressing continues and you begin to surface toward consciousness. Now you know you're no longer asleep, yet the caressing continues. Then it stops.

You open your eyes and a possum is standing there on your nightstand. You scream and rip off the sheets and blankets and rocket out of the room. You grab a broom and a bucket or whatever's handy. It's playing possum by this point, but you aren't an idiot. You eventually get the animal out of your house, and you don't sleep well again for a long, long time.

We, on the other hand, start typing, still *mmming* contentedly, because we have been given our daily allotment: a column idea.

6. Play Donkey Kong on the computer and wait for inspiration. It comes. "Pick up line three," barks your secretary. It's a guy with a yarn.

WORKING HIS BUTT OFF

We try to be a big-shot columnist, but there's apparently something about us that doesn't make the editors or readers all that confident about our ability to handle the high-profile stories. Especially crime stories.

All day long our colleagues are out covering serial killers and mob bosses, but whenever we try to get into the mix, the editors just pat our head and tell us to keep writing about where to get the best malted-milk drinks in the city and leave the hard stuff to "people with college educations."

Sometimes, though, when everyone's busy here at the plant, we're the only one a criminal can talk to, which was the case earlier this week when a scofflaw told us his story.

He doesn't want his name used, so we'll call him Jim Smith, which, in fact, is his name. We're not sure how he feels about having his age mentioned.

One afternoon last year, Smith, who is sixty-two, was driving down Seventh Street enjoying a cigarette. This wasn't the crime part. Smith wasn't smoking in a grocery store or a restaurant or a major league ballpark or anywhere near someone who would be harmed by secondhand smoke. He was driving alone and enjoying a smoke, which, when he was done, he flicked out the window at Ximeno Avenue. That's the point where Smith crossed the line from being a driver/smoker to a criminal, and you know how you're always saying where's a cop when you need one? Turns out he's following Smith around. He pulled the filter-flicker over and issued him a ticket. We sense your haughty applause.

Miraculously, "the officer handled everything extremely politely and professionally," says Smith.

Next, our man went to court where he was hit with a $100 fine for tossing the cigarette near Wilson High School's hallowed grounds. "Then," he says, "they toss on an additional $316 for 'penalties and assessments,' whatever that means."

Well, we explain, the $100 was a fine, the $316 was for other things, such as your various penalties and assessments.

As much as we dislike litterbugs, our thirst for revenge was well quenched by the $416 Smith had to pay, but the American Judicial System was not through with him.

"There was a mandatory eight hours of community service with Caltrans that I had to do," says Smith.

By now we're making a mental note not to take up

smoking again or, failing that, not to throw our cigarette butts out the window or, failing that, making sure there are no cops around when we do it or, failing that, taking up residence in a foreign country that has a rich and friendly ex-pat community, cheap Internet access and that doesn't cave in to U.S. extradition demands.

"So, I show up at the Norwalk Metro Station last week to do my Caltrans time," says Smith. Having apparently watched his share of prison flicks, he befriended a hardened public-service veteran, a gruff character working off a DUI fine by serving several weeks with Caltrans.

"I got there at 4:30 a.m., and it's about thirty-five degrees outside and there's about eighty of us waiting and finally four vans come. They hold fourteen people each, so they can only take fifty-six and everyone else is going to have to come back later," but Smith's new pal told him to hang around, because sometimes people get thrown off a van, which, sure enough, happened to some guy who broke the rules by bringing a cell phone to the work party, so Smith got his spot. This is the sort of thing that's now passing for extremely good fortune for Smith.

Next thing you know, you've got Smith raking and bagging "tremendous loads of trash" on the banks of the mighty Santa Ana Freeway.

"I'm on my sixty-two-year-old knees, ten feet from roaring eighteen-wheelers," he reflects, throwing numbers around like a math professor and claiming that those two hours were the best part of the five-hour job.

"They loaded us up again and we went to one of those areas of the freeway where we had to work at a forty-five-degree angle. They had me chopping tree limbs and actually sawing tree trunks with a forty-year-old unsharpened saw," he says. This was all done under the watchful eye of a boss named Boomer, who we choose to imagine as being played by Ned Beatty.

"Boomer was a good guy," says Smith, who bears no ill will against anyone at any step of his punishment. "I forgot to bring a lunch and Boomer shared his with me."

Throughout the course of his workday, says Smith, the workers took more than a few cigarette breaks.

"Seemed like we all smoked," says Smith.

And when they were done with their cigarettes, what do you suppose they did with the butts?

We know, and we could tell you, but we don't want to get Smith into any more trouble.

"I was dead by the time I got home that day," he says. "I don't think I could survive doing it again."

---

7. You're looking for a local angle on a national or international story, which, at the moment is the O. J. Simpson murder trial. You could go to the courthouse in LA and write about the media circus; you could even write, if things get really dry, about why they call it a media circus. That's your escape clause. "If it's a circus, where are the clowns? OK, bad example. Where are the Lipizzaner stallions? Where

are the flying trapeze artists? Where can a guy get a bag of peanuts?" A man calls from the *Detroit Free Press* and says he has a problem. *I don't do problems. Call your councilman.* I don't really say that, but I'm not interested, until he tells me his problem is that he's one of a half-dozen reporters allowed in the courtroom at the O. J. trial, and he can't make it today, and he needs a friendly columnist to take his seat for the day or else he might lose it for the rest of the trial. I am that friendly columnist.

A REPORTER'S TRYING TIME IN COURT

Friday, 6:30 a.m.: On the freeway early, cuppa mud bouncing on the dash, going to the O. J. trial as one of only twenty-four media people allowed in the courtroom. This, to me, an enthusiastic follower of the Trial of the Century, is great. After this little experience, I plan on being more difficult than ever to live with, peppering future columns and conversations with references to having actually been in the O. J. courtroom. I'll trump each speculative watercooler debate with, "Of course, having been there—as I have—gives you an entirely different insight into the etc. . . . " I am as happy as I've ever been.

7 a.m.: So I got to the Criminal Courts Building in downtown LA early. I'll just have another cup of coffee or two and wait till they start assigning the seats at 8:30.

8:30 a.m.: Up in the pressroom on the 12th floor.

It's like the first day in a new school for me, the only guy who doesn't know anyone. *Vanity Fair* correspondent and grouchy cosmopolitan writer Dominick Dunne is gabbing with author Joe McGinniss and AP's Linda Deutsch. Another writer is talking about how he's under contract to pen a few "think pieces" about the trial for *Penthouse* magazine. All of the media people are tossing in dollars for a pool to guess which juror Judge Lance Ito had booted from the panel on Thursday. No one asks me to play along. In fact, I'm informed that I've just cut to the front of the invisible hierarchal line for courtroom passes. After retreating to the rear of their silly little line, I score my *Detroit Free Press* pass.

8:55 a.m.: Back down to the ninth floor, where the O. J. courtroom is. After I deposit an embarrassing amount of pennies in a plastic tray, I make it through a metal detector with flying colors. Dunne gets through, too, after first ridding himself of a half-dozen $200 fountain pens. Outside the courtroom, scores of reporters are piled up behind a well-worn red duct tape line waiting for the jury to enter, so they can find out which one's missing. To no one's apparent surprise, it turns out No. 12 has been given the heave-ho. She was known to the reporters as "Touchy-Feely."

9 a.m.: Up for the kickoff. Either I'm really excited or it's just two hours' worth of coffee doing all the shaking. O. J. enters, and he's huge. He flashes a big smile, and the first thing I think is a reflexive, "Go get 'em, JOOOSE!" followed quickly by the sobering possibility that the mammoth man, especially properly

outfitted with rage and a knife, could dispatch me and a woman without leaving signs of a struggle.

9:15 a.m.: The as-seen-on-TV attorneys Marcia Clark and Johnnie Cochran perform one of their show-stopping debates, this one over whether the jury should be allowed to hear Simpson's taped statement to the police on the day after the murders. I decide Clark, who argued that the jury should not be allowed to hear it, is more persuasive. The Solomonic Ito sees it the same way.

9:45 a.m.: Those jurors yet to be jettisoned from the case for lying, kicking, getting homesick, or constructing lucrative book deals on the sly are brought into the courtroom. The latest addition, a seventy-one-year-old African-American woman previously known as No. 2457, is the new Juror No. 12. The entire panel looks like a collection of zombies. They don't laugh or smile or even exchange glances. They look like they hate one another. It's a mostly nondescript bunch, such as you'd maybe see on the return leg of a Las Vegas turnaround bus tour, save for a Latino in his thirties who sports a buttoned-up collarless white shirt under a black jacket with a foppish kerchief cascading from the front pocket, and a white woman, also around thirty, who looks a bit like *Married . . . with Children's* Christina Applegate save for an extraordinarily bad hairstyle that seems to be based loosely on the fountain in the men's room at the Madonna Inn.

10:10 a.m.: First and (as it turns out) the only sidebar of the day. These closed sessions are even more interminable live than they are on TV. While we sit around trying not to fidget, I can imagine the viewers at home being treated to a commercial for Amazing Blue Star Ointment on Channel 5. Jury remains sullen.

10:15 a.m.: Following the Clark-Cochran debate, the rest of the day will be given over to the defense's DNA expert, the fiery Barry Scheck, trying to show that LAPD criminalist Collin Yamauchi did a hurried and sloppy job with the samples taken from the crime scene.

10:30 a.m.: Fifteen-minute recess and not a minute too soon for those of us who drank a keg of pretrial java.

11 a.m.: More Scheck hammering away at the steadfast Yamauchi, who maintains a rope-a-dope strategy against the increasingly frustrated defense attorney. It's becoming terribly difficult to concentrate on the proceedings. There are forty-eight slim, rectangular light panels on the courtroom ceiling and forty-eight large, square ones. A clock on each of the four walls; nine hourglasses that I can see on Ito's bench; two remote Court TV cameras bolted to the wall above and to the jurors' right. The only thing keeping me awake is my fear of Ito, who rules his room with a piercing, sweeping gaze. I'd no more chew gum in his courtroom than I'd dress up like the Statue of Liberty and sing "The Lazy, Hazy, Crazy Days of Summer" at the top of my lungs, and still . . .

11:10 a.m.: JUDGE ITO YELLED AT US! Scheck was trying to get Yamauchi to define an "external blind proficiency test" (zzzz) and the criminalist asked the attorney to define what he meant, and the attorney said, "Well, why don't you define it for me?" and the criminalist said, "Well, if you define it for me maybe we can move along." Believe me, in the midst of DNA testimony, this interchange came across like Abbott & Costello, so we Twenty-Four laughed and tittered, at which Ito's left hand started jerking nervously like Captain Queeg's in *The Caine Mutiny*, and he stopped the trial to rail at those of us in the back: "This is not an audience-participation enterprise, folks. If I hear another outburst, I'm clearing the courthouse!" Pause to let this sink in while we bake under the hot glare of Sister Mary Ito's piercing stare. "There's nothing funny about this!"

Noon: Scheck's still trying to wear out Yamauchi with body punches, when the clock runs out for the day, ringing to an end my career as O. J. trial correspondent. Some day I'll look back on it and laugh, but right now I'm still afraid to laugh.

---

8. A poll comes out. These things can hit the spot when you're utterly idealess and there are no disasters in the forecast. Magazines, PR firms, websites, regular old bloggers, and even the occasional reputable researcher. They all release studies, polls, or popularity surveys that rank cities in numerous categories. I scan them regularly to see how Long Beach places. Sometimes we're No. 1! When that happens, I'm home and in bed before McDonald's has even stopped serving breakfast.

WALLETHUB'S RESEARCH
DOES A NUMBER ON LONG BEACH

You know what's a worse-run town than Long Beach? Fremont. Whoever runs Fremont couldn't run a carnival dime-toss booth if he was sober.

After Fremont, however, we've got no one else to laugh at.

WalletHub, a "social media site for your wallet," regularly accumulates data on America's sixty-five largest cities and releases rankings of the cities (best cities to retire, safest cities, etc.). This latest study, released Tuesday, puts Long Beach at sixty-forth, second from the Fremont-occupied basement, in the "Best & Worst Run Cities in America."

To spare you further suspense, the city you want to live in is Lubbock, Texas.

We're not mad at Lubbock. The fact that it's the birthplace of Joe Ely, Jimmie Dale Gilmore, and Butch Hancock alone speaks to the city's well-runness. Throw in the fact that it's the journalistic cradle of our friend and *LA Times* food columnist Russ Parsons (who's also pals with the abovementioned three musicians) and we are a huge fan of Lubbock, even though it's in Texas.

Texas, perhaps because of all its awl wells and awl refineries and awl money, is overburdened with well-run cities. According to the WalletHub report, seven of the top ten well-run cities are in Texas: Lubbock (1), El Paso (3), Dallas (4), Corpus Christi (6), San Antonio

(7), Garland (8), and the godforsaken city of Houston (9).

As smooth as Texas is, that's how rough-as-a-cob California cities are run, according to the Golden State–hating social media site for your wallet. California put up seven of the bottom ten cities. Besides Long Beach and Fremont, there's Riverside (63), Oakland (60), San Jose (59), Los Angeles (58), and Santa Ana (57).

WalletHub's smoothness methodology is limited to education (which gets the greatest weight), police and parks and recreation, none of which we can see having to do with smoothness of city running.

Long Beach Assistant City Manager Tom Modica said he didn't see any reason why the report should even be in the paper. We tend to agree, although Modica isn't charged with writing a column every day until he drops dead in the newsroom with women screaming and weeping hysterically.

In a written statement, Modica noted that Long Beach schools are not run by the city, and, at any rate, the LBUSD has been named as one of the top five school districts in the nation; that Long Beach is experiencing forty-two-year lows in violent crimes despite spending reductions; and that the Long Beach Department of Parks, Recreation & Marine was the Gold Medal winner last year for best parks department in the nation, "due in large part to increasing park space in park-poor areas of the city." (Because we're so transparent that you can read a book through our torso, we need to mention that our wife is a manager and application-writer for the Gold Medal competition, and she, too, took a moment out of our morning to mention the Gold Medal.)

Does Long Beach have problems? Probably. There's a pothole over by the Rite Aid by our house that can hold thirty-three Chilean miners, and there's still not a swing set in Rosie the Riveter Park, but other than that, we'll take a rough-run Long Beach over the smoothest city in Texas.

DEAR KIDS, WHOM DO YOU LOVE? MOM OR US?

To Our Dearest, Dearest Children,
Raymond & Hannah,

As you both know, we always plan for the future, our lack of even so much as a note scrawled on a cocktail napkin by way of estate planning notwithstanding.

More important to us than how much money you'll get when we pass on is which one of you is going to take care of us when we're too old to take care of ourselves, which could come as early as next Tuesday.

You almost don't have to say anything. We have the statistics here in our hand. It's a report commissioned by the Visiting Angels in-home senior health care, which is pretty much highlighted by the statistic that 70 percent do NOT want their parents moving in with them (the report capitalizes "NOT" to make sure there's no confusion about the surveyed adult children's lack of enthusiasm regarding the prospect).

OK, fair enough. As you've reminded us on more

than a few occasions, you never asked to be born. Neither did we. Nor did we ask to grow old, nor did we ask to have our wheels start to fall off to the point that we have to make purchases on that aisle at Rite Aid that you were both horrified to see when you were little and that sparked your first existential epiphany.

Not to throw your mother under the bus, but, if you were to entertain the idea of taking care of just one parent, would you at least consider the benefits of selecting us over Mom?

The Visiting Angel survey says no, you won't consider any such thing, or at least if you do consider it, you will dismiss it.

Assuming you're no more or less considerate than the adult children polled, if you were forced to choose one parent, only 33 percent would rescue us from the cold grasp of Visiting Angels, while Mom would be getting treated like a queen with a lap dog and cold cut sandwiches on demand.

Why Mom over, say, us?

In a broad and cruel generalization, 75 percent feel that dads have worse hygiene than moms. The same three-quarters of the paterphobic ingrates say we are more likely to say inappropriate things, 70 percent say we're sloppier and 68 percent say we're lazier than this mythical superwoman.

Eighty-six percent say that Mom is more likely than Dad to help with cooking and cleaning—that number seems a little low, but we're no Visiting Angel when it comes to the science of polling.

Seventy-nine percent say mothers are better than

fathers with the kids. (We have grandchildren?!) And 57 percent go with the idiotically overarching statement that Mom is "easier to live with," like we weren't already getting that impression from the preceding stats.

The survey turns toward bickering children, with siblings arguing like incipient divorcees over who shouldn't be saddled with the old man. While no one is thrilled (at all) with the idea of having sloppy, lazy, cussing, non-cooking and -cleaning Dad move into the den with his 19-inch RCA TV and a jug of gin, 32 percent say the kid who didn't move far enough away should "win" custody, while 27 percent say the booby prize should go to the child with the fewest responsibilities.

Finally, 72 percent of the respondents say they don't have a plan about what to do with us, and 54 percent say they haven't even talked about it.

And that, our dear children, is the point of this letter. We need to come up with a plan. We need to talk. We can change.

---

9. At a point fairly early in a columnist's career, one makes the startling discovery that life isn't like a river at all. Oh, were it like a river! Disappointingly, for a columnist, anyway, it's more like a Hula-Hoop: round and irritatingly repetitive. Some things that can't be avoided are holidays, which are not, in fact, holidays at all after the first fifteen Christmas

columns. Or the first zero Easter shoes column. They have to be dealt with. Pray for happy memories, because you're going to draw on a lot of them every holiday. And for God's sake, don't make the same mistake I did one Halloween when I dumped my entire frontal cortex of a lifetime of trick-or-treating into one column. What'd I think, there'd never be another Halloween?

A LIFE IN HALLOWEENS

HALLOWEEN, 1960: We're five. It's one of the cutest ages for trick-or-treating because greed has yet to supplant the weirdness of going up to strangers and asking them for candy, an act that flies in the face of everything a five-year-old has been brought up to believe. One minute our mom's telling us to never, ever, under any circumstances, take candy from a stranger—"because it might be filled with poison"— and the next she's shoving us up to a porch decorated with disembodied heads and exhorting us to go ahead and take it. "TAKE THE CANDY AND THANK THE MAN!" she hollers from the safety of the sidewalk when we hesitate. We got our costume at the end-cap impulse box at Iowa Pork Shops. It's that old-school kind that's a Vac-u-formed pirate's face held onto your head with hair-yanking rubber bands. It generates its own sweat. The gauzy suit part of the costume is made out of the same material that's favored by arsonists for its easy flammability. Our mom takes us around the block, a dog scares the hell out of us, and we get about thirty pieces of candy which we eat with a near-suffocating dread.

HALLOWEEN, 1965: We're ten. Old enough to understand that strangers give out unpoisoned candy because they don't want their outhouses tipped over or the windows of their flivvers scrawled upon with bars of Zest soap. In 1965 nothing bad ever happened to kids, so our parents were content to drink gin out of jam jars and watch travelogues about Rangoon on their Magnavoxes while their kids ranged unescorted over six ZIP codes, four school districts, and two temperate zones, collecting enough candy to survive the long and rugged winters ahead.

HALLOWEEN, 1968: Chicago riots. Kennedy and King killed. *Hair* and the *White Album* come out. Vietnam is on fire. Margaret Cho is born. This was the Halloween of our discontent. We're thirteen, as old as you can be and still attempt to go trick-or-treating. Maybe if our parents were more liberal with their allowance policies we wouldn't have to embarrass ourselves like this. Six or eight of us hit the 'hood as hard guys sporting decked jeans and white Ts. Old hags and grumpy men refuse to serve us, telling us we're too old and asking who we're supposed to be, anyway. Margaret Cho's dad, we tell them as we menacingly tap a candy "Marble Row" cigarette out of the pack. Just put the Pixie Stix in the bag, Pops, and no one's outhouse gets tipped over.

HALLOWEEN 1975: A couple of years into college and people are urging us not to be a fuddy dud—that was the hip lingo back then: "fuddy dud." Come on! Didn't we want to put on a funny and ironic costume and go out dancing and drinking at a fun Halloween costume party? Nah. On Halloween all throughout our high school and college years, we were always in what kids back then used to call "the doldrums." They didn't understand us. For us it was never about the costume or the going out. It was always all about the candy.

HALLOWEEN 1990: In a desperate attempt to breathe life back into the grand old lady of kid-based holidays, we and our friend Dave Wielenga rent out Bogart's, a popular LB nightclub, buy a bunch of beer, book a bunch of bands (including Chuck, a Charles Manson tribute band that featured Lovingkindness' frontman Tom Holland on vocals and about fifteen other musicians, such as us, making a racket in E minor), and peddle a load of tickets for a Bad Taste Halloween Fes-T-Ball. There's also a great potty-mouthed comedian named Sammy Seagull there. It's a great time, and it's exactly what the fundamentalist anti-Halloween extremists were warning people about.

HALLOWEEN 2001, A SPACE ODYSSEY: OK, now who's the mom taking her kids around the block, exhorting them to take potentially poison-laced candy from strangers? We are. We are that mom. Actually, or technically, our wife, Jane, plays the part of "Mom," and we star as "Dad" while we join every other overly protective parent in the Prestigious Plaza in squiring fire-retardant kids around pre-screened neighborhoods. Among our crowd is the cop across the street, who makes us feel safer because he can shoot at anyone who frightens us, although no one wears the costume that would frighten us the most, which would be a costume portraying Our Life With Two Children & Its Attendant Responsibilities & Things That Can Go Wrong!

HALLOWEEN 2007: Our first Halloween in more than a decade and a half without taking at least one of our children out trick-or-treating. We watch some old show on TV with our wife and make wry observations regarding "Fun Size" snacks.

It dawns on us, when the doorbell rings and we hear the chattering of costumed kids on our porch, that we get out of our chair like Wilford Brimley and, once launched and semi-erect, walk like Walter Brennan in *The Real McCoys*. (We feel as old as that reference.) Maybe not that bad, but that's what it seems like, dagnabbit. And it dawns on us, too, that we live in the same style of house, in the same neighborhood through which our mom once escorted us on this holiday. And it dawns, further, on us that these kids are us a long time ago, and the parents are us just a couple of years back. It's nice, in a lot of ways, living in the same place your whole event-packed life. Sometimes change is bad, not good.

We toss some Twix in a pint-size pirate's pillowcase. The boy buccaneer spins to leave.

"THANK THE MAN!" the mom hollers.

10. Carpe diem, whatever the diem may be. When you've got absolutely nothing, just Wikipedia (the verb) the day and you'll find that it's National Something Awareness Day or that some food advisory board has declared it National Advised Product Day. Or Week or Month. It can be as simple as a sandwich.

THE MONTH WE HAVE A SANDWICH

It's National Soup & Sandwich Month, as if you couldn't tell by the snap in the air, by the sight of the leaves turning opulent shades of gold and crimson, by the fact that, well, the food tastes better.

Now, here we are, bellied up to the counter of Subway, gnawing our way through a Footlong roast beef sandwich with everything. We always order it that way at Subway, yet invariably the chain's helpful sandwich-builders pose the question afresh with each item as they crab their way along the assembly line: "Bell peppers?" Yes, everything. "Salt and pepper?" The works, please. "Onions?" If you've got it, slap it on. "Salad oil?" Look . . .

It's a couple of bites past noon and the Subway on South Street in Long Beach is doing a boffo business. And it's no wonder. The stats are in from last year, and, according to Oscar Mayer—the company that took it upon itself, along with Campbell's Soup and Kraft Singles cheese, to proclaim September as National Sandwich Month—the Long Beach/LA area ranks No. 4 in sandwich-eating, behind Philadelphia,

Baltimore, and Pittsburgh, but ahead of Long Island and Seattle, which attained its ranking, no doubt, thanks to the migrant Angelenos who took their sandwich-eating ethic with them when they fled Southern California.

The Subway shop is showing great restraint in not exploiting the fact that it's National Soup & Sandwich Month. There are no special banners hanging from the ceiling. The employees aren't wearing "Kiss Me, I Make Sandwiches" buttons. In fact, no one seems to know that it's National Soup & Sandwich Month.

"No, I didn't know that, but the manager is on vacation this week," says manager pro tem, Bawa Kumar.

"Does the owner always take National Soup & Sandwich Month off?" we ask, imagining a blindingly white strand along Puerto Vallarta peppered with celebrating soup and sandwicheers and their spouses.

"No, I don't think so, but you really should talk to him. He'll be back next week."

There is no time to wait. We're already more than a half-dozen lunchtimes into National Soup & Sandwich Month, and if the Long Beach/LA area has any chance to ever hit the No. 1 spot in sandwich consumption in American cities, it should start bearing down right now.

We're having roast beef, we think we mentioned. "What are you having?" we ask the gentleman behind me in line. He looks away and never gets very close to us again. Which is too bad, because our follow-up was going to be what he thinks about sandwiches. So we ask a woman, Sandy Daniels, who was having a turkey sandwich before catching a movie in the theater next door, how she feels about sandwiches (after first breaking the ice by telling her that our dad had a dog named Sandy. Died the day we were born.).

"I think they're great," she says. "They're cheap, easy to eat, and they last a long time, and now I won't have to fill up on popcorn at the movies."

Even though soup shares the billing with sandwiches this month, we don't ask Sandy, or anyone, what they think of soup. Who eats soup? Soup's something you get with a meal. It's a culinary accessory. You eat soup when you're sick. You eat soup when you don't want anything to eat. You eat soup when you live someplace where it's freezing nearly all year long. The Long Beach/LA area doesn't even show up on Campbell's Top-10 soup-slurping burgs. Spokane, Washington, leads the list, which also includes such arctic locales as Grand Rapids, Michigan; Green Bay, Wisconsin; Minneapolis-St. Paul, Minnesota; Des Moines, Iowa; and Buffalo and Albany, New York.

Eventually, we waddle out of Subway, overfed and sleepy. A foot's an awful lot of sandwich to eat, but we do it for the old hometown, because, just like most competitions, the sandwich-consumption game is a game of inches.

---

11. There are inevitable columns. Besides holidays, there are annual events that require columnizing every year. In Long Beach, the main event is the

Grand Prix, where racecars rip up the streets of Long Beach while a couple hundred thousand race-watchers wander the circuit and buy meat.

WHAT'S BETTER THAN BREAKFAST ON A STICK?

People whose jobs include coming up with the occasional assignment for us had two ideas for our Grand Prix coverage. One was to spend the entire day walking around the racecourse wearing women's high heels so we could find out what it felt like to be Miss Toyota Grand Prix of Long Beach. The second was to eat every kind of food that was for sale at the race.

Next thing you know, we're standing in front of a Philly Cheese Steak kiosk in front of the Convention Center on Friday morning with a soggy cardboard carton of chili cheese fries in our hand, trying to holler above the roar and whine of Le Mans cars.

"What you wanna do is you don't wanna fill up on hot dogs or fried stuff straight away," we told our friend and assistant eater John, the brother of the Cop Across the Street, who was going at the $6.50 chili fries way too avidly, considering the long day of eating we had.

We tossed the fries and strolled over to the SMG Savor booth to have the most important stick of the day: Breakfast on a Stick.

Generally, we feel that there is no kind of food that can't be improved by a stick, but in this case, we were disappointed. It was merely a breakfast sausage done up corndog style. It could've used some bacon wrapped around it, but it was only $3, so we weren't crippled with the disappointment.

"Maybe we need a rule," suggested John. "Don't buy food that's cheaper than water."

It's a good rule, and it pretty much held up throughout the day of eating. Water, at most places, sold for $3 to $4. Almost everything you'd want to eat cost around $10.

After walking at a brisk clip through the Lifestyle Expo in the Convention Center, we emerged near the Silvio's booth. We were still fairly hungry, so we were a sitting duck for the booth's boss Silvio Correa, an extremely friendly and enthusiastic Brazilian who came up with the recipes for the race crowd.

"The chicken is my creation!" he crowed sort of like a mad scientist. And it was a good creation. Ten bucks gets you a mess of it, or, even better, the calabresa sausage, or, better yet (everything we had at Silvio's was better than the thing we had before), the fresh green salad with the Ipanema dressing. It was the best food we'd have all day.

"I grew up in Brazil," said Silvio. "This kind of food is what I make for my friends in my backyard."

We chased the Silvio fare with, finally, a hot dog. Not the kraut dog or the $8 sausage sandwich. Just your basic $4.50 hot dog. Served at one of the many SMG Savor booths, it was an utterly serviceable hot dog. "It's the best one in all the compound," said server Claudine Hallahan. Each Savor stand benefits a local charity or school group. A percentage of our hot dog money went to Millikan High School's JROTC.

A bit farther down the way, between the Convention Center and the Arena, was the dauntingly titled Fat Boy's booth. With its gaudy signs and a boss who was roughly three times our size, it looked like a good state fair type of place. And if you like state fair food a lot, this would be your kind of chow stand. We asked the big boss what's best. "Well, our burgers are pretty famous."

Famously bad. "Worst I ever had," we said to John after one bite. "Want some?" we offered, handing him the $7 culinary failure.

We crossed the track using the Toyota bridge that dropped us behind the straightaway behind Grandstand No. 29, where we saw a gigantic big-rig-turned-barbecue theme park called Juicy's Outlaw Grill. We were absolutely unable to resist buying the $9.75 barbecued turkey leg, which is about the size of your niece and came grilled to about 20 minutes past perfection. The thing was drier than British humor, and we had to look around for a while to find a trash box big enough to hold it.

Juicy's also sold an $8.75 Giant Western Sausage that was alarmingly long and sort of assaultive-looking, and a half-pound Outlaw Burger was yet another option. We hope to one day be half the man that Juicy's seems to deem as its core demographic.

Less threatening was the nearby Angel's Heavenly BBQ, run by friendly and happy family members who follow festivals around out of their home base in Norco. We sampled most of their offerings and would merrily recommend the marinated chicken sandwich, or anything made with the Cajun-style Andouille sausage.

We also liked (and believe us, we were getting mighty picky by this time as we waddled from booth to booth) many of the things on sale at the Brander's BBQ booth, behind grandstands 30 and 31. The pulled pork was a lot better than the tri-tip, and—though maybe this was our now severe lack of hunger speaking—the $8 rice-bowl treatment would be the way to go, either with the pulled pork or the unadventurous Farmer John's Polish sausage.

We had grown mighty tired of barbecue by this time, so we were happy to see a King's Taco booth as we neared the end of our trek, behind the No. 27 grandstand. We couldn't eat another thing, so we had the soft taco, which, at $1.75, was cheaper than gum. We asked John if he wanted one. "Hell, no!" he shouted over the semi-loud celebrity-filled Toyotas. We got the carnitas. "You want the onions and red sauce?" asked the cook.

"Yes," we said, because we imagined that we did. He looked doubtful, but put on onions and red sauce, which, whatever it was, made our eyes pop out of our head and our mouth explode, and our heart leap out of our chest and run around like a headless chicken. We made a beeline for the nearby lemonade stand, which, surely because of its proximity to King Taco and its naive red-sauce-ordering clientele, was getting $4 for unrefrigerated bottled water. We drank the bottle in one shot, which caused the fire to dim enough for us to tell John that it was time to leave.

And, besides, our feet were killing us.

12. It doesn't always have to be funny. Humor is my default mode when faced with anything ranging from a shrimp cocktail to old and obscure wars (in warfare, anything less than 100 years old is too soon). But there are subjects that strike me as being gag-proof, and suicide is right up there. It seems like I've written way more than my share about people killing themselves, from friends to the famous.

A TIME TO REFLECT ON THE POETRY AND LYRICISM OF SUICIDE

Our grandmother, who we loved so much it still breaks our heart, said a couple of weird things after she reached 100 years of age. One was, "Mexicans are happy people. They carry their babies in baskets," and the other was, "I love everything you write, but I think the things I like most are when you write about suicide."

Not that she was suicidal herself. She waited patiently for 103 years before she died in her sleep at home in 2007.

We have had some good friends who have ended their lives at their own hands—who hasn't?

And, of course, there are the suicides by people we don't know, but whose works or lives we've admired. Robin Williams is only the most recent, and his suicide shook a good portion of the country, assuming Facebook is representative of the entire country.

We weren't a big fan, so we managed to not get

emotionally wrapped up in Williams's death as much as we did with the suicides of David Foster Wallace and Vic Chesnutt.

Chesnutt, in particular, was all over the subject of suicide in his songs, and we've always found his "Florida," in particular, of some catharsis and solace.

The song is great in the first place just for the fact that he writes about the state, "There's no more pathetic place in America." But of suicide he sings, "A man can only stand what a man can stand. It's a wobbly, volatile line," and "I respect a man who goes to where he wants to be, even if he wants to be dead."

Chesnutt also tackled the British poet Stevie Smith's beautiful and haunting "Not Waving But Drowning," setting the short poem to music. It's a lyric that seems perfectly suited to Williams's suicide with the subject of a man's distress not taken seriously by others until it's too late. The dead man in the poem "always loved larking," say the narrators. They reckon the water was too cold; that his heart simply gave out. But the dead man responds:

Oh, no no no, it was too cold always . . .
I was much too far out all my life
And not waving but drowning.

There are few serious poets who haven't tackled the subject—everyone from Brautigan to Whitman, Coleridge to Bukowski. For a wordsmith, it's a sadly easy subject to tackle.

We prefer the subject set to music, and there's a

huge body of work on the subject by songwriters as well as more florid poets.

Song lyrics are typically more straightforward than purer poetry, but sometimes, it's best to tackle suicide straight on, as Jackson Browne did in "A Song for Adam," or as John Hiatt did in his song about his wife's suicide in "Right Now" ("One cigarette missing from my packet/You must have thought about it just that long").

Our grandmother, who could recite from memory dozens of poems—she used to recite at the Hotel Virginia for the pleasure of old ladies drinking tea—was partial, from our columns, to Lucinda Williams's "Sweet Old World," about her brother's suicide. It's a touching litany of "what you lost when you left this world," and it concludes with what survivors almost invariably feel: "Didn't you think anyone loved you? Didn't you think you were worth anything?"

---

13. There are no days off for your columnist. There's simply not enough material occurring between the work hours of 9 a.m. and 6 p.m. Even at parties. You need to mine the off-time, too. Can't I just forget about the column for a couple of hours at a party? I cannot.

WHEN NATURE'S HORROR SHOW PREYS ON THE MIND

We love nature because of its refreshing lack of tragedy and horror.

Last weekend, we were having dinner at the home of our friends Charlie and Wendy in Long Beach's bucolic and wildlife-overrun Far East, and we were listening to Wendy's dad tell a story when a look of revulsion came over our face because, while he was telling his story, we were watching a falcon pulling long strings of viscera from a bird it had pinned to a tree branch.

Of course, we had to direct everyone's attention to it because no one wants to watch a bird being eviscerated alone. You want to do that with friends and family. It's fun!

So, we were all enjoying the show, when a mockingbird, which we all took to be the slaughtered bird's mate, began screeching and dive-bombing the falcon, and we humans down below began sobbing and wailing over this sudden and apparently tragic turn. We could deal with nature when it was simply predator vs. prey, but when you throw a grieving widow into the mix—especially one seeing its spouse EATEN ALIVE!—well, it all becomes too much to bear.

The party, now well sapped of its joie de vivre, nevertheless continued as we picked halfheartedly at our, we're abashed to admit, chicken.

The following day, however, Charlie let everyone

know that, after further examination of the scene, the slain bird was not a mockingbird at all but, rather, a dove—"a very old dove with no relations that was really sick anyway," he assured us—and that the dive-bombing mocker was just trying to either get in on the action or move the falcon out of the neighborhood.

Either way, we felt much better and had chicken again the next evening.

---

14. **Help your kids with their homework. Not algebra. Remember, you said you'd never need algebra for the rest of your life. Now's not the time to back down on that promise or prophecy. My daughter had to do a report in high school on something to do with World War I, and I had to write a column. Seems like we could make a father-daughter day out of this. She got an A on the paper, and I wrote one of my favorite columns.**

DULCE ET DECORUM EST

We couldn't keep the headstone clear of the mud and rain.

It was cold, as cold as it ever gets here, and the leafless trees provided no more shelter from the glancing rain than an umbrella that's lost its fabric, leaving only exposed ribs.

We were underdressed and undershod. My daughter wore a now-drenched hoodie and jeans; I was sloshing about in a pair of loafers that were never going to be usable again after this. And the two of us were lost in a sea of dead people.

The site was the Long Beach Municipal Cemetery, right next to the older Sunnyside Cemetery on Willow Street. My daughter, Hannah, was doing a high school project on World War I, and she decided to center her assignment on people in Long Beach who served in the Great War, as it was called. It certainly wasn't called World War I at the time, because it was to've been the War to End All Wars. A war as horrific as the Great War doesn't dare imagine a sequel.

Hannah wondered if there were any veterans of the war alive in Long Beach who we could talk to. I explained the math and the actuaries. The only vets from the first World War we were going to commune with were here at Long Beach Municipal and other places much like it.

We found out a couple of days later that one U.S. veteran of WWI, though not a local boy, had still been alive, though we only found out on Sunday, when we learned that West Virginian Frank Buckles, who had enlisted at sixteen and was the last living doughboy and grappler with the actuaries, had died at 110.

The grave marker we had been trying to keep clean enough for a photograph, without much success—we lacked any tools, where a stiff broom or even a sturdy rag might've done the trick—stood vigil over the body of Frank Dean O'Neal, born June 1890, died January 1970.

In *Long Beach in the World War,* a book compiled

by the American Legion in Long Beach in 1921, we discovered that the young O'Neal was born in Lyndon, Kansas, enlisted in B Company, 316th Ammunition Train, 91st Division, and was sent overseas July 12, 1918, and was stationed in France at Cherbourg, St. Ammont (probably Saint-Amant), Billom, and Saint-Nazaire. He was discharged May 13. Married Grace Hess, September 3, 1917.

In the *Press-Telegram,* many Septembers later, a small item noted that Frank and Grace celebrated their 50th wedding anniversary. Grace, the article tells us, was a 1916 Poly High graduate. Frank, we learned, "is a well-known California highway and trucking contractor."

Frank Dean O'Neal's grave marker, in its necessary economy of words, distills the deceased's achievements as:

"Cook. US Army
World War I"

We used our hands and battered loafers to scrape enough soaked earth away to read even that much. Hannah took some pictures of the marker, and we marched off to find more.

Almost everything's ineffable at a quiet cemetery like Long Beach Municipal—the sadness, the sacredness, the serenity. And we were all alone with our daughter, the only two people on the living side of the lawn, bending against the wind and rain. Oh, the discomfort! Could anyone have had it worse than us at this moment?

We remembered the gist of a letter written in Bourges, France, during Thanksgiving 1918, from a young corporal, Charlie Swift, to his father back in Akron, Iowa.

It's a long letter, and we only know of it because Cpl. Swift writes of meeting Hannah's great-grandfather, also of Akron, Iowa, on the streets of Bourges. Swift had been fighting on the front lines for seven months when a shoulder wound sent him to a hospital in Bourges.

"Yes, father, I think I have done my little bit in this old war," writes Swift. "I have been in some of the worst battles that have been fought. I was on five different fronts and have witnessed some of the worst sights that could be seen. . . . It's pretty hard to see your pals that you have eaten with and slept with get knocked off.

"I think it has done me good. I don't think I will ever have reasons to crab again at anything that goes wrong . . . "

With that thought, we stopped crabbing. We held our daughter's hand and soldiered on. It's no problem at all. In fact, it felt like an honor.

And, anyway, a little rain never killed anyone.

15. Worst case. A disaster that's so monumental that it alters the course of life in America. One that makes everyday life jump its banks. Severe catastrophes will jarringly determine how a newspaper writer's day will go. On September 10, 2001, I had a

rare pre-planned column. Bob Dylan's album *Love and Theft* was coming out the next day. I would swing by the store and pick up a copy, give it a few listens, write a review of it, and be home by 3 o'clock. Instead, came September 11's events . . . My editors wanted a column about how television was dealing with the news as it was coming in (although I did drop by the record store to buy Dylan's CD. You can't let terrorism push you around). So, all day, it was me and the remote, flicking from one horror to the next.

SOME WORDS ROSE ABOVE THE TALK

Anytime there's an American tragedy as profound as Tuesday's attacks on the World Trade Center and the Pentagon, people turn to TV, where, on Tuesday, they were reminded repeatedly that there has never been an American tragedy so profound.

Peter Jennings on ABC, Tom Brokaw on NBC, Dan Rather on CBS, Aaron Brown on CNN, and all of their far-flung correspondents, experts, and eyewitnesses struggled with "devastating," "horrible," "horrific," "horrendous," "most terrifying" "most frightening"— every negative superlative in the lexicon of tragedy, only to find that the words that meant the worst had been squandered on events that didn't match up to the epic proportions of Tuesday's assault on America.

Only a few comparisons came up: NBC's Brokaw called it "the most serious attack on the United States since Pearl Harbor" and Fox's Brit Hume noted that the 1995 Oklahoma City bombing "was once considered the worst tragedy in U.S. history and that (Tuesday's events) absolutely dwarfed it."

The pictures served to take the place of the unspeakable: the jetliner slicing into and exploding out of the south tower; bodies falling, people jumping, bystanders screaming, survivors reeling and hobbling covered in blood and dust; rescue workers poking dejectedly in stunned silence amid the inconceivable rubble. Somewhere in there, maybe, you could find the words to describe how this event burned and slashed new trails into the already viciously scarred geography of terror, but no one was using them on the air Tuesday.

Also left unspoken throughout the day was speculation on the number of dead. All of the networks tiptoed respectfully around any figures, only mentioning in the most somber of tones the number of people who usually work in the Trade Center and the number who generally visit daily. And, of course, the passengers and crew on the planes, and the rescue workers ambushed by the second tower crash.

The magnitude of the tragedy was ably illustrated by CBS's Bob Orr, in Washington, who reminded us that jetliners are "basically flying bombs, carrying as much as 20,000 pounds of fuel" and "when any one of these crashes anywhere in the world, it's a tragedy of major proportions."

While the back-to-back attacks and subsequent collapses of the Twin Towers replayed constantly like nightmarish video wallpaper in screen insets or on anchors' backdrops, the major networks and news channels dominated the hundred-plus-channel cable universe all day long.

In addition to finding news at the usual places on the dial, you could find CNN on its sister and subscribing channels, such as TNN and TNT; ABC popped up on all of the affiliated ESPN channels; NBC came up on PAX; CBS was picked up by the music cablers VH1, MTV, and CMT; MSNBC with Brian Williams was carried by the shopping channel Shop NBC; and Fox could be found on all of its properties, including the Health Channel, the Fox Movie Channel, Fox Sports, and Fox Family.

Admirably, most shopping channels dropped the hard-sell for the day, with such mercantile channels as America's Store and QVC suspending regular programming, offering prayers, and sending out sympathy to the families and friends of those affected by the tragedy.

Local news teams tailored the Tuesday events to their own regions. Reporters from Los Angeles channels spent much of the day at Los Angeles International Airport, where three of the four hijacked planes had been scheduled to land.

More notably, KTTV reporter Jeff Michael turned in a haunting report from the ghost town that was downtown LA.

Less compelling were stories turned in by reporters sent out to interview disappointed tourists being turned away at Disneyland and other Southern California fun zones.

We were invited to watch all manner of news conferences with Los Angeles city and county officials, and Long Beach/Signal Hill's Charter cable system carried a conference with Mayor Beverly O'Neill, Long Beach Police Chief Jerome Lance, Fire Chief Skip Beck, and others.

Other regions keyed on matters of local interest as well. If you tuned in to Chicago's WGN, you'd find a reporter reassuring viewers that the Chicago White Sox, in New York to play the Yanks, were staying in a hotel far enough away from the Trade Center. The team was fine.

The Internet was slow on Tuesday with people trying to go deeper than TV for information on the attacks. It was tough to come by, though, thanks in part to TV's excellent coverage. The search engine Google, in fact, carried a message telling Web surfers, in effect, that if they were looking for news, watch TV.

If you wanted to voice your own opinion on the matter, however, there was room on the Net for everyone's opinions. Chat rooms were abuzz with the airing of views, and visitors could add their own or respond to such disparate message lines as "Nuke Every Middle East Country NOW!" and "This Is Clinton's Fault" and "Let There Be Peace on Earth."

CHAPTER THIRTEEN

Mothers.
Birth, Step-, and Grand

You write columns for a certain number of years and the daily snippets start to weave together as your sprawling memoirs. Way out of chronology of course; a biographer would have to puzzle them together like someone reassembling a love note that's been put through a shredder.

There's no way for anyone but the most diligent readers, really, to make any sense out of my early youth, with my two-and-a-half mothers who I don't always name and for whom I rarely use the birth- or step- prefix in columns. So, let's see if we can put some of these strips of that aspect of my life together.

The first time my mother's name was printed in the Long Beach newspapers was her and my father's wedding announcement in April 1953. Her name was

Mina, but she went by her middle name, Joanne. She was twenty-two.

The accompanying photo showed her attired in candlelight net and lace over ivory satin. The bride and groom would live in Long Beach after a honeymoon in Del Mar.

By January the couple had two children, a girl, Debra, born on Valentine's Day ten months after their wedding, and me, eleven months after that. They were on pace for twenty or twenty-five kids.

Less than a year after I was born, she appeared in the paper again—this time on the front page.

"A Long Beach woman died, her husband was critically hurt and their baby injured Friday afternoon in a crash on Pacific Coast Highway south of Capistrano. Two others were killed.

"Two cars and a huge tanker truck were involved in the accident which scattered crushed victims and twisted wreckage along a stretch of road north of San Clemente."

On September 16, 1955, my mother and father had taken Debi and headed down the coast to help their friends move. Because, at ten months, I wasn't going to be able to do any heavy lifting, my parents left me with my grandparents. Mom was driving because my dad had just gotten off his shift at the Richfield refinery.

Somewhere between San Juan Capistrano and San Clemente, she drove the car into oncoming traffic on

Pacific Coast Highway and crashed head-on into a tanker truck.

After the initial collision, the tanker swerved across the road, killing a middle-age couple from Needles.

A couple of days later, a coroner's jury found our mom guilty, relying on testimony of a man who was driving behind her when the accident occurred. The last paragraph: "The jury's formal finding at the inquest held at a San Clemente mortuary was that the tragedy was caused by Mrs. Grobaty's 'own negligence.'"

So many questions remain, but now there's no one around to ask. I've read the three newspaper clippings dozens and dozens of times looking for clues, and I'm always almost finding them. If only the reporter would add one more sentence.

Eventually, starting in 2007, little bits came to light.

PHOTOGRAPHIC MEMORIES

What I know about my mother couldn't fill this column. I know she was born in Compton. I know she died in 1955, the same year I was born. I know she died in a Page One wreck on Pacific Coast Highway in which two other people died. I know that she was pronounced dead in San Clemente. I know her name was Mina, but that she went by her middle name, Joanne.

I don't know what kind of life she lived. I don't know

if she was happy giving birth to two children in eleven months. I don't know if she was planning on having a dozen or more. I don't know if she could cook or if she was athletic or if she was possessed of a merry, chirping laugh or a horsey guffaw. I don't know how she ranked, 1 or 2, on my father's All-Time Favorite Wives List.

I asked him once during those tact-bereft preschool years—maybe I was four—as our Fairlaine descended into a tunnel beneath a Long Beach Airport runway, which one he liked better, my real mom, or this one, waving my hand dismissively at the woman riding shotgun, my freshly minted stepmother.

The answer was ambiguous, delivered in the form of one of those violent twisting-around beatings administered by most dad drivers of the fifties. It ended any dreams I had of becoming a pollster, and I don't recall asking my dad about any preferences thereafter.

Nor did he ever speak about my mother. Nor did I ever see any pictures of her, save for a wedding photo, in which she looked happy enough, but that was Day One of her life as a Grobaty. I never saw any other evidence of her for half a century. She was always a bride in my memory.

A couple of weeks ago, just before I took a vacation in San Clemente with the family (a mom, a dad, a boy, and a girl, just like my folks; and don't think I don't think of car wrecks every time I go to San Clemente), I received an e-mail from Lois Sarver, who had been going through some old photos that belong to her aunt, Edith Owen.

"We came across some pictures that might be of interest to you," she wrote.

I drove to Edie's house in Long Beach and her niece Lois answered the door.

Edie was delighted: "You look so much like Joanne!" she exclaimed clearly, through all the oxygen tubing that is keeping her relatively comfortable in her final stages of emphysema.

Now eighty-nine, Edie had worked with my mother at Williams Diamond Shipping Co. during the early fifties. My grandfather, Ray, had worked there as well and had introduced Joanne to his son, my father.

Edie had also been a bridesmaid at the ensuing wedding, and now, fifty-two years later, despite everything, she's still easily recognizable as that attendant.

She told me stories about my mother, how nice she was, how friendly she and her parents were to Edie, how much she enjoyed holding me when I was born, and she handed me photographs, one by one, each filling in some hole in my life that I hadn't really noticed before. Many of the photos were of a vacation at our family's cabin on the north shore of Big Bear Lake, long since sold.

There was my mom, snuggled in a rocking chair next to my dad (and Edie on Pop's other side) in front of the fireplace. My mom snuggled! And another of her falling in the snow outdoors. My mom fell! In the snow!

And more: one in her nightgown, another wedding shot, with the full party, including my granddad, a couple of snapshots taken around the cabin's kitchen table, another with the gals around the fireplace. There's even a wallet-size photo of the long-cherished wedding picture.

I can't tell you how strange it was to catch, suddenly, these glimpses of my mother after all these years. I'm not even sure how my dad, who has, like my stepmother, passed on, would react. I mean, I don't think he'd hit me or anything, but it always seemed like Joanne and her tragic and sudden death was a part of his life he wanted to forget about.

With me, it's different. It's a part of my life I've always wanted to know more about. And now, thanks to Edie and her photos, I do.

SAY HELLO TO OUR LITTLE FRIEND

You wouldn't think we would be writing about a ukulele. At least we wouldn't think that. We've always thought that the ukulele is to string instruments what the kazoo is to wind instruments.

On Sunday, we were lazing around in the pool at our old house, which now belongs to our sister, Debi, and we were talking about the estate sales that her husband runs.

We have always been after her to alert us to vintage guitars that might pop up on the sad occasion of someone's death; sadness would go away in a big hurry for us if the deceased left behind a 1968 Martin D-28 that we could pick up for $60 because its strings are old.

"We never get old guitars," said Debi.

Then she said she had a Martin ukulele.

"A Martin?" we yelped, splashing around frantically like you're not supposed to do when there's a shark nearby but which we would anyway because it's the natural thing to do when there's a shark or a Martin stringed instrument in the vicinity.

"Yeah. I don't want it. You can have it. It belonged to our mom."

Now we're all "whaaaaa???!!!" because among the thousands of things we didn't know about our mother, the biggest was the fact that she used to play a ukulele.

"Yes," said Debi. "A guy she was dating before she met Dad bought it for her in Honolulu."

We shot out of the water like an orca. Mom dated someone before she met Dad? Suddenly everything we thought was right was wrong. Who was this mysterious serial-dating, ukulele-strumming person who left us when we were a baby with nothing more than our stunning good looks?

So, in a matter of minutes, we were the new owner of one of our favorite possessions, which came in the highly unlikely form of a ukulele.

It's a beautiful instrument, made of mahogany (koa would have been nice, though sound pops better out of mahogany; koa is prettier and mellower, and in any event, inheritors can't be choosers) and decorated a bit with ivoryoid binding. We are suckers for ivoryoid binding.

And the binding is what promotes the Martin to a

Style 2, much more desirable than the mousey Style 1 and preferable, to our taste, to the barely fancier Style 3 and even the flamboyant and gaudy—and rarest of them all—Style 5. There is no Style 4. There is a Style 0, but it's so plain and unremarkable that you can snap them up all day long for only $600. We wouldn't play a Style 0 with Tiny Tim's fingers. That's how much of a ukulele snob we've become in the last seventy-two hours.

We've also aligned ourselves with some cool ukuleleists in hopes of distancing us from the Tiny Timmish stigma attached to the instrument. John Lennon, George Harrison, and Paul McCartney have all played the uke (though the smart money would've been on Ringo being the sole uke-strumming Beatle).

Also, William H. Macy, spaceman Neil Armstrong, fair-minded rich guy Warren Buffet, Marilyn Monroe, Greta Garbo, and Elvises Costello and Presley.

Inside the ukulele case was a piece of paper with lyrics written in lovely handwriting. We like to imagine our mom gently strumming the ukulele, her long black wavy hair cascading down her left shoulder as she softly sang to us:

This is the moment
Of sweet Aloha
I will love you longer than forever . . .

But she never did. "Hawaiian Wedding Song" wasn't even translated into English until 1958, and Presley didn't have his hit with it until 1961. Our mom died in 1955. There are some aspects of math that don't totally baffle us.

So, in the intervening years, someone else was monkeying with our uke, to say nothing of what would've been a better ending to this column.

In fact, we don't know what songs our mom played on the Martin. Maybe she didn't play it at all. Could be she just put it up in her closet, or, better, in her hope chest, saving it against the day she could give it to her son. Yeah, we choose to believe that.

So, thanks, Mom (and Debi).

I don't have any memories of my mother. I only remember feeling somewhat special about not having one when I was little and living with my grandparents, both of whom still worked at my granddad's tuxedo shop. I was left in the care of nannies during the daytime. One was Hawaiian and the following one Scottish, leaving me in my formative language-learning years with a Scottish burr, and urging my grandma to "Come, Grrrrandma! Look at the birrrrrdies!"

I remember that when I was three or four, I enjoyed the awe and shock of other kids when I told them my mother had died when I was a baby. What did these children have of any interest in their lives to tell me? Nothing.

There is one odd memory that I have that I swear

is true, and it goes back to before I even knew how to talk.

Thirty years later, I incorporated it into a screen-play I cowrote called *Eyeballs In, Eyeballs Out*.

> ### HENRY
> *Do you even remember your mom?*

> ### TRIPP
> *Not really, I guess. I was a baby when she died.*

He pauses, decides to go on.

> ### TRIPP
> *Sometimes it seems like I remember being in Granddad and Grandma's house and there were a lot of people there dividing all my mom's stuff up. Relatives, I guess. And I started crying when this one woman took these two little porcelain angels who would be kissing when you put them together. I didn't want anyone to take them away, but I couldn't talk. I didn't have any words, so I just yelled and cried and was frustrated that no one knew why.*

Meanwhile, I lived for about four years with Granddad and Grandma Bet and old Bapa, my great-grandfather, who I only recall as a man who got up every day and put on a three-piece suit and a fedora, even if all he had planned for the day was a walk around the block. He would come up to me while I was playing outside and fish around in his pocket and come up with three or four pennies. "These have been slowing me down," he'd say, handing them to me, usually with a piece of Black Jack licorice gum. Three doors down the street on Keever Avenue was Grandma Bet's mother, Great-Grandma Pritchard.

For all its roots in tragedy, I can't imagine a better early childhood, and I don't know that there was ever so much love heaped on a child. When my dad remarried, I continued to spend as many weekends and as much of the summer as I could staying with my grandparents on Keever.

When I think of the total, blissful comfort of kindness and devotion, I invariably think of my grandparents and my great-grandmother.

IN LOVE WITH A CENTENARIAN

Look: Here's my favorite picture of myself.

I'm about a year old, fully swaddled in late wintertime clothing, one foot tenuously planted on the ground, the other taking a less than confident stride—my first step in my life, weaving my way between an orange tree and an avocado tree—toward the best woman I've known.

You can get in a lot of trouble calling one person the best woman you've ever known, but I say that confidently and with full awareness that the other women I know closely would gladly and readily agree that they've never known another so full of goodness, intel-

ligence, joy, sympathy, comfort—especially comfort—
and all the other suddenly feeble-sounding superla-
tives I could drag out of Roget's.

The woman in the picture (you have to look closely;
she's hidden behind the avocado leaves) is my grandmother, Laura Elizabeth Grobaty, or Betty, as she's
preferred, or Grandma Bet, as she's known by her six
grandchildren, of which I am the only one who can
also claim—brag, more generally—to be her son.

My mother was already four months dead when I
took my first step in the backyard of my grandparents'
house on Keever Avenue under the flight path of the
deafening Douglas DC-7 prop planes that cracked
plaster and rattled windows on their descent to Long
Beach Airport.

Grandma had a fuller plate than most women will
ever have: working at her husband's formal wear business on Atlantic, helping take care of her son, who
lived with his grandmother—my great-grandmother—
just down the street; taking care of her father-in-law
who also lived in the Keever house with me and
Granddad, working in local politics (she was an alternate delegate at the '64 Republican National Convention in San Francisco), and all the time making me
feel safe and loved in what must have been a weird
world otherwise.

There were nights when I was eight or ten when I'd
rub her feet and listen to her tell me that a time would
come when I'd be too busy for her. I'd have a life of
my own, she'd say, and I wouldn't come and visit her
as often. I insisted she was wrong. How could there

ever be a time when I would prefer anything to sitting by Grandma Bet's side playing cards or watching her cook while I sat at the cherry wood table that's now in my family's house? It was all I wanted out of life; I could do it forever.

And yet it came—not the fact that there were places I'd rather be, but places I needed to be. I visited much less frequently when my grandfolks moved to Laguna Hills, and only occasionally after my grandfather died, and only twice after my father died and Grandma Bet went to live with her daughter in San Jose.

Still, we talked frequently on the phone. When I felt blue or had troubles, I instinctively would think to call Grandma Bet first, not so much to burden her with my problems, but to just take that long-familiar comfort from her company as we bickered lightly over politics or discussed pronunciations and definitions of words.

Today, four days after her favorite holiday, is her 100th birthday. I, predictably, missed the weekend get-together in San Jose—although my son and I went to her 99th there last year.

I'll give her a call today and we'll talk about the same old things, and I'll feel refueled once more with the comfort of love afterward.

But it's a conflicted feeling I have on Grandma's milestone to end all milestones. She's never wanted to live to 100, and I can see why: It's an overly long trip—she's buried two sons, seven siblings, at least two, maybe three generations of friends.

I know what she must be wishing for herself when

she blows out the candle on her cake tonight, and, despite my selfishness in always and forever wanting her on earth with me, I hope she gets her wish easily and elegantly.

She knows where she's going in the next life, as does everyone who knows her and believes in heaven. And, because of my time spent with her here in this life, I know exactly how she'll feel when she gets there.

A decade after Grandma Bet died, I found out more about her. Sometimes it seems as though my life is like a paint-by-numbers craft that takes a whole parallel lifetime to finish. And every few years a new color is supplied, and I manage to fill in all the No. 6 spaces in the piece. This came while I was finishing this book:

PEEKING INTO OUR GRANDMA'S BOOK OF DAYS

"I have a present for you," our slightly older sister Debi told us on Sunday.

We like presents; we're not like everyone else.

"What is it?" we asked, as everyone idiotically does instead of just waiting a second.

She smiled. "You're really gonna like it."

Great! We like getting things we like. She took us into what was her bedroom when she was growing up. Now she owns the whole house, and she just uses her old room for presents and other things.

She handed us a diary for the year 1955. "It was Grandma Bet's," she said, needlessly, because we instantly recognized our beloved grandma's handwriting.

Our sister, who possesses most of the family's history in its various forms of photographs, letters, and ephemera, has been steadily parceling out our past to us. This diary was the latest installment, detailing our grandma's life in the year of our birth.

It was busy, that's what our grandma's life was in 1955. And fairly repetitive. Up early, go to Mass, spend long days at her husband's new formal wear shop, take her mother on errand runs, buy groceries, make dinner, and then to bed.

There were occasional teas and club meetings, card games, and watching *I Love Lucy.*

A lot of feeling low, unappreciated, insufficient, guilty, fretful, unloved by my granddad. We could suddenly understand her appreciation and sympathy regarding suicide.

There were some high moments—attending the Miss Universe Ball, going to the cabin on Big Bear Lake, visits with relatives. But a lot of the diary really brought us down. She had a lot on her plate, and we weren't even born yet, which would add considerably to her workday later in the year.

We were quaking with anticipation when we finally brought ourselves to read about that glorious day.

January 12, 1955: "Jim (our dad) called from the hospital—Joanne (mom) went in at 3 a.m. At 1:30 p.m. he called, Hello, Grandmother, you have a grandson! Eight pounds, 13 oz. Timothy John. Not so pretty as his sister but a very fine baby."

OK, wait. We're confused. Confused and a little irritated. Grandma, who was a master of the English language, didn't put any quote marks in this entry. Obviously, our dad said, "Grandmother, you have a grandson," but did he keep on talking up to and including the part about us not being as "pretty" as our sainted sister, or did he stop at "grandson" and our grandma added the utterly unnecessary commentary regarding our relative attractiveness and our mere serviceability?

All of that belongs to the ages now. Anyway, it's all forgiven, especially since we've long surpassed our sister in the prettiness category.

The diary ends suddenly and sadly in the summertime. Our mother died in a car crash in September.

We know, anyway, that Grandma, just fifty-two at the time, suddenly, in addition to her usual chores, had to take care of her son, badly injured in the crash, and her ten-month-old grandson.

You can only imagine what that must have been like. In Grandma's book of recollections, with every event otherwise described and chronicled, September, and everything after, is blank.

A strange bit of confluence masquerading as coincidence is the fact that my future stepmother, Gertrude Elaine Hauck, was working as a secretary at the *Long Beach Independent* (which ran, more or less, the same stories about the wedding and the accident as its competitor, the *Long Beach Press-Telegram*) at the time those articles about my mom were published. Maybe she saw them, however briefly: "Oh, nice dress." "Oh my, horrible accident. That poor family." Then have another sip of coffee before turning to her favorite comic strip, Pogo.

She would quit her job when she married my father four years later. I would start my job at the then-merged *Independent, Press-Telegram* twenty years after the accident.

Something I'm still not clear about was that at some point during my first four years, my dad took off for Maine. I don't know why Maine other than, perhaps, it was the farthest he could get from the life that had literally come crashing down on him.

And I know that his father eventually flew out to Maine to bring him back, scolding him that he still had a family, and it was time to man up and shoulder the awesome responsibility of being a single father.

So he came back. He began dating Elaine (like my mom, she scrapped her first name, Gertrude), who would become my stepmother.

She was delightful. We all went to the zoo in San Diego one day—one of those trial dates, I imagine, to see how we'd all get along—after which I showed my appreciation by throwing up my lunch, gaudily colored by a bottle of grape juice I had downed (then upped).

My next memory was of them getting married, and of my crying in rage because I wasn't invited on the honeymoon. Who doesn't like to go on a honeymoon?

With Granddad's help, they bought a house on Vuelta Grande in the new Eastern part of Long Beach, and just like that we were a family.

I know it was wrenching for me at first, being taken away from my mother and father who were my grandparents. But I was still at the age where change is the status quo: You have a mom, she dies, you have new parents of a sort, and you're taken from them to start a new life with an acquaintance of a father and his new wife who you're told to call Mom, one who unironically frequently sings around the house, "*Que Sera, Sera* (Whatever Will Be, Will Be)." Another favorite, and we're not sure how much irony was imbued in her rendition, was her singing "The Prisoner's Song."

If I had the wings of an angel
over these prison walls I would fly

It was fun for a while. I know my stepmother loved me sometimes. She liked to laugh when everything was going right, and I was good at making her laugh.

She was a near-cultish Marianist, praying the rosary almost incessantly—in the bathtub, in the car, in bed. She would frequently call my sister and me in from playing on the block in the afternoon, draw the drapes to darken the room, and we'd kneel on the carpet to recite the Five Whatevers—Joyful, Sorrowful, Glorious—Mysteries, five rounds of ten Hail Marys with The Lord's Prayer between rounds like a devotional ring girl at a boxing match.

She was arbitrary and generous with her discipline and denials, and she cooked like food was a punishment. It sometimes seemed like it was a triumph for her to concoct something that brought fear and dread to us at the dinner table. Weeping was not an unusual response from me and my sister, and even Dad.

And she was as strict and unbending as a women-in-peril prison warden. Our bedtime, for more years than it should have been, was 7:30 p.m., a particularly dreadful time to be in bed, especially during the summer months when it was still light out and we could hear our friends carousing outside.

I suppose it would have seemed normal to me and Debi had we not had the pleasure of frequent weekends at our respective grandparents' homes, respites that seemed like shore leave during wartime.

Why am I being so coy about all this? I missed my real parents, Granddad and Grandma Bet. Now it was all turn off the TV, don't listen to Vin Scully on your transistor radio after a bedtime that was so early that nocturnal creatures were still in deep-REM sleep. Don't read after bedtime.

My stepmom didn't get up to make my sister and me breakfast on school days. She slept, or at least remained in bed, until we were gone. Our dad made breakfast; my sister made lunch. An angry, bitter, resentful lunch, invariably bologna—on at least one occasion not even bologna, but, rather, the picture of the bologna that was on the cover of the packaging.

On weekends and summer days, our stepmother wouldn't even let us in the house.

"Bravo," I can hear today's idiotic parents saying. "Make 'em go outside and play and use their imagination. No video games! No TV!"

Yeah, and no bathroom, either, Dr. Spock.

Mom (I never called her stepmother. It seems weird doing it now, which I'm doing for mere clarification to separate her from my birthmother. No such clarification was necessary in my time spent at home, when we never, ever, broached the subject of Joanne) fielded frequent calls from neighbors saying, "Did you know your son is peeing in the bushes?"

Dad, on the other hand, was a cheerful, gracious man, who got married, yes, out of love—he was absolutely devoted to my stepmother, at least until the very end when everything started coming off of everything at once, with his physical health nose-diving alongside her mental health—but also, he would tell me much later in his life, because he needed someone to raise the children well.

"Oh, well, nice try," I semi-assured him shortly before his death.

I didn't take to Dad immediately, either, upon his

return from Maine. Again, I was more of a Granddad man.

I was sort of wary of the whole new parental lineup, maybe even especially with Dad being back in the picture, until I almost got killed in a train robbery.

WHEN MY FATHER BECAME MY DAD

Suddenly a gunshot rang out . . . but I'm getting ahead of myself.

I wasn't overly impressed with my dad for the first few years of my life. It's a little hazy what he was even up to for a while back in those days when I was busy learning how to walk, how to say a few words, learning to sit and stay—all the basics. I don't remember him being around while that was going on.

In the car accident his injuries were so severe that the family delayed Mom's funeral for a few days, waiting for it to be a double affair, but Pop pulled through and after a year or so in rehab—throughout which I grew up a bit, increased my range of mischief through the newfound mobility following my first steps—I'm under the impression he left town for a while, leaving me to the care of his parents, and my sister to our mom's parents, while he did whatever it was he felt he needed to do to get on with his life.

I learned to call my grandparents Mom and Dad, and I remember even then knowing it wasn't entirely accurate, but I had to call somebody that and they were the ones doing the mom-and-dadding at the time.

Eventually, my dad came back—it's a long story that I don't know—and he remarried when I was four and life began again with, depending on how you're keeping score, my second or third mom and a revamped version of my original dad.

I'm told that I was fairly cool toward the new arrangement. I do remember a little about the wedding reception. A cousin—a new one, from my step-mother's side—snapped my suspenders while a jazz band played onstage at the Petroleum Club. I cried when the bride and groom drove off in a borrowed funeral hearse for a honeymoon, leaving me back at Square One, at the grandfolks' house, for another two weeks, which was fine. I liked it better at my beloved grandmother's and grandfather's, anyway.

Eventually life got back on the more traditional track, with a new home in the boomtown of Los Altos on Long Beach's east side, except I still wasn't having much of my dad, and I certainly wasn't calling him Dad. I don't remember if I called him "Hey, You," or, "Hey, Yellow Shirt Guy," or what, but he had begun to worry about it. What would it take for a son to acknowledge his father? He did what he thought he was supposed to do: Bought me baseballs and a glove and played catch with me in the backyard, hauled me around with him in the car, took me up to the cabin in Big Bear, but still no "Dad."

Perhaps he was still trying to prove his fatherhood and its attendant title and respect when he took the family to Knott's Berry Farm one late spring afternoon. It was my first trip there, and I loved it. It was, for me, a real visit to the true West. Maybe a little too true for a lad of only four. I was sitting in a car on the train that ran through Knott's, maybe a couple of rows away from Yellow Shirt Guy and my stepmom, when suddenly a gunshot rang out.

Sweet Lord Jesus, as my granddad always said, we're being robbed! Bewhiskered men peered over the bandanas that mostly hid their faces as they shouted and shot their six-shooters into the air, causing all manner of calamity before stomping into the next car to spread their terror.

When the smoke cleared, I was in the safest place on the train, on Dad's lap, holding on and trembling as he held me in his arms—they were just regular arms, but at the time, they seemed huge and unfailing. Utterly impenetrable by peril or panic.

And that's how I spent the rest of the train ride, wide-eyed but secure, pinned and made fairly immobile by Dad's arms that didn't let me go even after I'd calmed down. In fact, I'm sure they tightened a bit.

My faith in my father was completely restored on that ride, though I wonder if that shiny new faith would have been shaken a bit if at that moment I had managed to twist around and looked curiously at the tears on Dad's face.

It's easy to wallow in exaggerated oppression and paint a childhood in a torturous palette, setting things up neatly to show what one has bravely risen above. You can't run for office without it. Mine wasn't, in sum, a bad childhood. Most of the misfortunate flaws of my stepmother have long since been reduced to jokes between my sister and me.

Dad coached my Little League team, played endless hours of catch with me, took the family out for Sunday drives. In little breaks from her strict and draconian disciplines, our stepmother joked with us, made palatable meals on our birthdays, at least (it was a culinary event to be cheered when she made spaghetti without straying from the instructions on the Lawry's spice packet), and she even threw the occasional party for us, though entertaining wasn't nearly as entertaining for her as being entertained. I was in the Cub Scouts precisely as long as it took before her turn came around to host the den of a dozen boys at her house.

My folks loved cocktail parties, and they were the typical sixties "Mad Men" affairs, with highballs first, followed by little cups of liqueurs considered swank and socially savvy: crème de menthe, Benedictine & Brandy, Tia Maria. My sister and I spent many evenings tossed onto strangers' beds at these parties, being aroused at 1 or 2 a.m. and slumped over, groggy, and confused, in the backseat while our parents inevitably sang in the front: "Show me the way to go home / I'm tired and I want to go to bed / I had a little drink about an hour ago / and it went right to my head."

Not long before she died, in one of her irritable highs that came with severe and never-ending bipolar bouts, my stepmother told my sister that we kids got in the way of a lot of fun she could have had. She couldn't have children of her own, and my feeling was she felt marrying into a family would fill that void. And it seems that she felt a grievous mistake had been made.

Still, there were moments when she told people (though rarely me) that she was proud of me after I became a columnist. She kept a few of my articles, though she was also critical of a lot of them. She was given to calling me at work (my coworkers knew when she called because my head would hit my desk in despair) and saying, "I'm cracking crab right now."

"That sounds good," I'd say warily.

"On your column. I'm cracking crab on your column. Where do you come up with this garbage?"

In those later years, the wild swings between depression and manic highs came while my father's health was deteriorating rapidly. She could see that the party was over. She bought clothes like mad, filling my sister's and my vacated bedrooms, the closets overflowing onto the beds; the dressers overstuffed. Hundreds of blouses, dresses, and sweaters, and she was stuck on a complaint of having nothing to wear. Our dad planned a lifetime dream trip to Ireland and England, which eventually had to be cancelled because of his wife's depression that was fixated on her lack of attire.

Sometimes, she would stop whatever she was

doing and stand in one place, frozen, staring at something in the far distance, unable to decide whether her next move should be to the right or to the left.

Dad was suffering from several health problems at once; a weak and torn esophagus, bad kidneys, a bad liver, diabetes. When he finally got well enough, briefly, to come home, my stepmother said she couldn't deal with him, so his own mother, my Grandma Bet, then in her nineties, took him in at her home in Leisure World in Laguna Hills.

Eventually, he died. A long, horrible process with months spent at UCLA Medical Center, with intermittent stays in other hospitals and an array of nursing homes and rehab centers. My sister and I spent twelve hours at his bedside on his final night and morning in hospice at a place on Fourth Street.

Our stepmother got measurably worse. She bounced back and forth in a frenzy of consumption, buying cars, computers that never came out of their boxes, new carpets and drapes every few months. And lows in which she dabbled constantly with suicide. More dark humor. She took several pills, most past their expiration date and was rushed to the hospital. That was the first, jarring attempt. Eventually, they became tiresome and predictable and thoroughly draining on my sister and me. She sat in her car in the garage with the engine running, but left the side door to the garage open. She took a few halfhearted cuts to her wrist. She sat on the railing of the second floor of a building at Cal State Long Beach until the campus police picked her up and we came to spring her from the campus pokey. She perched on a bridge over the Los Cerritos Channel until some God-fearing people from the nearby mobile home park found her, dragged her to their house, and prayed over her until we arrived to pick her up. If you added up her 5150s, you'd get into theoretical numbers represented by Greek letters.

Unable to deal with her anymore, my sister put her in an assisted living home, where she continued her ups and downs. One day throwing a cocktail party in her room for her fellow residents, the next leaping from her balcony into the bushes below. The latter put her in the hospital. I refused to visit her. Two weeks later, I got a call in the middle of the night from an aunt telling me that my stepmother had died. Then, I went back to sleep.

My sister and I and a few other family members cleaned out her room in the assisted living center. Not much there, a little bit of furniture, a few trunkloads of clothes, a box of knickknacks that included a wind-up rabbit all dressed up in a blue dress. None of us had seen it before. For kicks, I wound her up and set her on the balcony railing. She sang something in German for about thirty seconds, then hopped twice and fell to ground below, in the smashed bushes where our stepmom had landed days before.

It was good to hear us laugh again.

CHAPTER FOURTEEN

So Happy I Was Sad

The poet Philip Larkin wrote in "This Be the Verse," his most famous work: "They fuck you up, your mum and dad. They might not mean to, but they do."

Like many parents who had less-than-idyllic childhoods, my wife and I were determined to fuck up our kids in a totally different way than how we were fucked up.

We eschewed virtually all discipline stricter than a raised voice or a show of disappointment. We cast aside the bromide that "they need a parent, not a friend." We spared the rod and enthusiastically spoiled the children: a boy, first, who we named Ray Charles after my grandfather Ray, and Jane's father Charles. It took a few hours before we realized we had given him the name of a black and blind soul singer.

Six years later, we had a daughter, Hannah Carroll, honoring Jane's maiden name.

Nothing in this life has brought me so much joy than my two children. There have been times over the years when I was aware of the goodness of the present moment. Once, when I was sitting on the grass in front of my high school, I had the little epiphany that everything was good and right. I had amazing friends, few pressures, enjoyable classes, splendid nights and weekends.

The other epiphany was a serial one that came frequently as my children were growing up. I always wanted to stay in the present, even as year after year shoved us all into newer presents with the future pulling us. Much of the time I was so happy I was sad, dreading every single passage as the children grew. The worst was kindergarten, when they march, practically full-fledged adults, into the auditorium singing "It's a Hoopity Hey Kind of Day!" in their cardboard caps and mortars. For both our children, it was the era before phone cameras, which was great for me. I could bury my head in the videocam, tears filling up the rubber cup of the viewfinder.

For a working dad, I was extraordinarily lucky. Typically, there are no set hours for a newspaper columnist. The assignment every day was to write a column by deadline, which, during the course of our career, ranged from 1 a.m. for the next day's paper, to 9 a.m. for a paper two days later. At any rate, I was there for Ray and Hannah in the morning, getting them dressed, feeding them, getting them off to school or daycare, and picking them up at the end of their days.

Roddy Doyle wrote in one of his novels words that hit us hard, saying of one of his characters: "If he thought of it, the fact that he didn't have children any-more—if he'd been an actor, it was what he'd have done to make himself cry."

I knew at the time how magical it was, and I never wanted it to end. The years came at me like enemies.

TIME PASSED

I have to be careful around my daughter, Hannah. She tries so hard to please her old pop that she can get intense and crippling headaches trying to perform the impossible.

On Tuesday, the day before her last first day of school at our neighborhood K–8 institution, I had to keep her from shrinking in size and time-machining herself back five or six years, where I wanted her—and, let's face it, where I wanted to be too.

"Where is my little third-grader?" I fake-wailed. "Where is my girl with the little white socks and pleated jumper running around the track in the Bunny Hop?" Of course, I have to say all this while hugging the current, nigh-on-eighth-grade version of Hannah as hard as I can because I am such a sucker for my kids that nothing else matters much to me.

Anyway, a few hours later, she was tearing up a bit

and worrying because she was unable to scrunch herself back to the third grade, and it fell to me to assure her that there was no one who has walked on this planet, nor is there anyone in line to do so, who I love or will love more than I love her right now as a big girl.

And, so, sleep came, and time passed.

On Wednesday, I got Hannah up as I have for the last eight years—and if you throw her brother, Ray, who's now in college, into the mix, I've been doing this for one or the other or both for fifteen years; waking them up, cheering them up, going through the backpacks and parent permission slips, combing their hair and tying their shoes (I don't think there's a thing I've done more than tie children's shoes), making breakfasts and lunches, driving them off to school, kissing them good-bye, and shoving them off to learn whatever it is they're going to learn from all these teachers, both inspired and inspiring and, to varying degrees, less so. Teaching is a profession and like all the noblest professions, there nevertheless are those who are unhappy with their lot or have grown sick of it. On the first day, we all go, parents, teachers, and students, hoping for a year of brilliance and optimism and cooperation.

(And in terms of daily chores, I don't mean to come across all heroic here. Our hardworking wife handles the later-in-the-day chores; the homework, the teacher conferences, the purchasing of clothes and supplies, ramrodding the big projects, and learning algebra and medieval history along with them. The fact that she has to be at work earlier than I do and the fact that she doesn't write a column puts her in a bit less of a glorious and blinding spotlight here.)

We paused Wednesday on the porch to snap a photograph of Hannah, an annual ritual, and then off to school for another first day.

The scene is eternal: The sad and nervous kindergarten parents, usually both Mom and Dad, before they streamline the process to where just the one is needed for opening day.

The all-polished-up first- and second-graders, smelling of freshly sharpened Ticonderoga #2 pencils and undulled, unsnapped Crayolas.

The odd mom with the cartons of cupcakes making the rest of us look like bumbling louts.

The dads, either wearing messed-up contractor T-shirts or executive three-piece suits, all talking ball with one another and acting like it's nothing to get all sentimental over.

The teachers, all enthusiastic and friendly, while expertly evading those parents who have a stunning number of gripes to make even before the opening bell.

The perpetually besieged office staff trying to handle a thousand questions (many hyper-repetitive: What time does school get out?) and field demands (many undoable: How do I get my kid into Mrs. Crabapple's class?).

The principal presiding as always—shouting out a million remembered names and helping out as a valet for kids clambering out of the tank-size SUVs still favored by soccer moms everywhere.

The pitch-black playground, freshly tarred and newly painted with the icons of the playground—the hopscotch squares, the boundaries for hoops, kick-ball, tetherball, and four-square, the cakewalk for the various carnivals and fiestas, the outlines of all the states of the country.

The final hugs and kisses, all embarrassing to vary-ing degrees, depending on age and gender and num-ber of witnesses.

The friendly honks despite the signs prohibiting it (there are signs barring dogs, gas-powered model planes, and peyote, too; you have to pick your spots).

The overall friendliness, in fact, of the whole homey Rockwellian scene. The waves, the winks, the reac-quaintings, and at last the watching of Hannah as she disappears into her clutch of friends—the ones not too popular, not too unpopular, she informs me. The Mama Bear set.

And so concluded my final first day of school at the elementary level. I'll miss those annual openers, but I still have all the rest of the days this school year to treasure, right up till Hannah's eighth-grade gradua-tion, with all its pomp and promise and—and watch me cry like a fool over this one—the finality of that last day of one long and happy era.

ALMOST GROWN

We were with our daughter at the Starbucks in Albertsons on Tuesday morning, because coffee tastes better when it comes from a giant and faceless corporation, when we noticed a couple of cakes decorated for graduation.

That's when it dawned on us, if "dawned on us" means the jarring epiphany felt like being clamped in the jaws of an orca, that our daughter, Hannah, had roughly the shelf life of a cake remaining in her high school years.

We waited for our $8.50 worth of two coffee drinks.

"When is graduation?" we asked her, with the unreasonable hope that she'd say, "In 2022, Dad."

That'd be great. That would mean we still have more years left of Dad's Donut Days at her elementary school tucked inside our little Plaza neighborhood. It would mean more science projects, like the one where we bought a half-dozen brands of microwave popcorn to see which ones had the most/fewest unpopped kernels. It would mean hundreds of afternoons walking her home from school with her backpack slung over our shoulder and our young dog, Jimmy, bounding along ahead of us.

"June 13," she said. As in three weeks and one day from now.

That's not enough time. Not nearly. Three weeks and one day will go by as quickly as this sentence. Bam, period, full stop.

You can purr your platitudes at us all day: The best years are still coming, the most rewarding part of being a parent is seeing your children all grown up, the blah blah, yakkity yakkity yak . . .

We recall talking to a therapist once, who held his hands in one of those therapeutic steeple shapes while musing, "Do you think the fact that your children are growing up could be a contributing factor in your depression?"

"Contributing" might be too weak a word, otherwise, Bingo, Doc. I see that our time is up.

But not before he did the "best years are ahead" riff.

We don't buy it. The best years are sleeping on the floor of your child's room when she or he has the flu or a fever. The most rewarding part is scuffling around in the kitchen, still 90 percent asleep, scrambling eggs or making smoothies or dropping a couple of frozen waffles in the toaster and getting the kids' clothes out and ready and strapping them in the car and singing snippets of Disney songs and quizzing them on what movie they're from.

Too quickly comes a mess of plateaux. Kindergarten graduation, eighth-grade graduation, 10th birthdays, 13th birthdays, 16th birthdays, 18th damned birthdays. Our son, Ray, six years older than his sister, ran point through all these milestones. We still remember holding a video camera tightly against our crying eyes at the kindergarten graduation as the little kids sang to their parents. Good Lord, that was a crushing day. Hearing those kids sing "Hoopity Hey" made "See That My Grave Is Kept Clean" sound like "The Beer Barrel Polka."

So, yeah, three weeks and one day before we sit with our wife and son on cold aluminum seats at Millikan's football field, holding a video camera, a newish one that's too small to cover our face, waiting for a thousand graduating students to pomp-and-circum-stroll to their seats.

"We feel sick," we told Hannah at the Starbucks counter.

"How do you think I feel?" she replied.

That was nice of her. That made us feel better.

RAY AT 21

Our son, Ray, liked just about everything when he was little. "This could be mine," he would suggest or declare while admiring, what?—a blender, a mini-vac, a magnifying glass, a pair of glasses, an umbrella.

One of our favorite pictures of him, and we'd share it with you, but it's all yellowed with age (already!), is of Ray—Corky as we wound up calling him for no good reason—when he was maybe four years old, walking down the sidewalk away from the camera and our house, wearing a gigantic sombrero and holding on to a helium-filled balloon by a string. He looks utterly satisfied; a boy with every possession imaginable.

Today, Ray Charles Grobaty turns twenty-one and breaks our heart all over again. We're not, as it turns out, cut out for our children's rites of passage.

We weren't even sure we were cut out to be a parent twenty years ago and a lotta change when our two-week-old son fell off the bed of our grandfather, his namesake, while we were in the dining room talking to our grandmother. We heard a *thunk* and raced into the bedroom to find Ray (the younger) squalling on the floor like a baby.

The next day, we found blood in his diaper and rushed all over the place to find out what sort of irreparable damage the fall that was all our fault had caused, the whole time thinking, *We were stupid to ever think we could raise one of these things. We can't even have a bike for six months without pieces flying off.*

But everything was fine. Who among us doesn't have blood in his diapers now and then?

So we set out to be a father, whatever that means. We took a lot of time off work so we could be a stay-at-home dad, which is a weird thing to be, because when a stay-at-home dad takes his toddler to the park, all the stay-at-home moms shoot glares at him thinking he's hired a baby as a prop to troll for romance. Shoot, it'd be easier and cheaper to just use a Ferrari.

We fled the park scene and ended up going places like the Bolsa Chica Wetlands to look at the blue herons and snowy egrets and black skimmers and least terns.

One morning when baby Ray woke up crying at 4 a.m. and couldn't stop, we put him in the car (we always drove our kids around when they cried) and drove down to Newport Beach to share a bagel and watch the sun come up, turning the sand beneath the receding surf dark orange, over which ran the silhouettes of darting curlews and dowitchers pecking frantically before the next wave. We remember it like a postcard.

When the time came that we needed to go back to work full time, forcing us to put Ray into day care, we bought lottery tickets like mad hoping to win millions so we could just all live together in a compound somewhere near Big Sur and never have to face a problem again. We won a couple of free plays. We would have problems to face.

But they were nothing, the problems. Raising Ray, as well as his little sister, Hannah, whose recent entry into high school didn't do our heart any good, either, has been nothing but a pleasure and the sort of joy we never thought possible, and it's a strange joy that comes tempered with terror, worry, heartbreak (heartbreak over every little thing that goes wrong), and the eternal feeling that, still, we're stupid to have thought we could ever raise one of these things.

So, anyway, yeah: twenty-one today. A man, just like us, except a hundred times better. He's made us exceedingly proud and, while we're pleased with how he's progressed, a huge part of us wishes we could win a lottery—not one that pays money, but one that would make Ray and Hannah little tots again so we could enjoy life all together one more time.

Ray's a couple of inches taller than us, now, too, but are we any different from other parents in seeing him still as we remember him best, little again, sombrero'ed up and jauntily sporting a bright balloon, going off on an adventure of his own making—just a few steps from the corner. A few steps, and he'll be out of sight.

HANNAH AT 21

We have surrendered to the enemy that is time. Just gone limp and let it drag us around in whatever direction it chooses, which invariably happens to be relentlessly dead ahead.

When we and our children were younger, we would rail against time, most remarkably at the various milestones: graduations at every level, 5th, 10th, 18th birthdays—all sad and beautiful occasions.

On Monday, our beautiful baby girl Hannah turned twenty-one, and we just didn't have the heart or fight to rage against the clock and calendar. Our son, Ray Charles, hit all of the key dates six years ahead of Hannah, so her 21st birthday is pretty much the last of them. For once, and finally, we took it well, like equanimity is our middle name.

The old us would spend the day in despair at the thought of our little angel reaching full-fledged adulthood when just moments ago she had been planting her face in a slab of chocolate cake on her 1st birthday.

The new mature, or perhaps just resigned, version of Hannah's Dad loaded her into the car Monday morning and, after a swing by Starbucks, drove down the coast to Fashion Island to turn her loose on, what our friend John D. Wilson terms, "that Temple of Conspicuous Consumerism deep in the OC."

On the drive we listened to her songs, Mumford & Sons, Foo Fighters, Snow Patrol, and chatted like old pals. We haven't been a textbook dad, never put any stock in "she needs a father, not a friend." We have eschewed discipline. Hannah's never been on restriction, never had her iPhone confiscated. We tell her anything of ours is hers, which results in us losing everything. We come upon something cool and show it to her. "This is mine," we declare. "Can I have it?" she asks. "Yes," we say, handing it to her.

So, she's spoiled, is she? She is not. Our wife and we have trouble ferreting out her wishes sometimes. When we shop with her, she looks for bargains or just tells us she doesn't want/need anything.

She was less demure on her birthday jaunt. It's a good thing we care nothing about money. We went to Lush, a shop that deals in hand-crafted soaps and related products. A Lush lady squired her around the store describing every single product, and Hannah tossed stuff into a basket and checked out with a hundred-and-something dollars worth of Lushness. A coal miner uses less soap.

"Where do you want to go next?" we asked.

She didn't know.

"How about a new bag?" we suggested. She was good with that. We went to Kate Spade and found a suitable purse for just $350, dropped another couple of hundred at Anthropologie, another $50 at a dog store because she wanted treats for Jasper and Annie (it's thoroughly disgusting what dog treats are made of nowadays: lamb trachea, for God's sake, and worse).

We were game to spend more (it's insane how much money we have), but she couldn't bear it any longer.

We gabbed some more on the drive home, and, later, we went out to dinner at 555 with the whole family. We shared a bottle of a nice Stag's Leap table wine and toasted our daughter's latest milestone. We didn't feel like sobbing even once. We don't know what's wrong with us. Must be the meds our doctors have thrown at us. All we felt was pride, happiness, and love.

CHAPTER FIFTEEN

Politics and Religion

Oh, what could go wrong writing about politics and religion? Of all the subscribers I've lost at the newspaper because of reader outrage, most have come from political crackpots—a nice and convenient overarching term for those who disagree with me. It's also a rich source of hate mail, which is another well to which we turn when we're not overrun with talking dogs.

I was raised in a devoutly Catholic and perhaps even more devoutly Republican household.

You can go back to my great-grandmother to find people deeply involved in Republican politics (although our great-grandmother, whom we had the pleasure of knowing and loving into our teen years, was also a fighter for women's rights, which made some of her detractors mutter darkly about her sexual leanings, a muttering that was stifled by the fact that she had eleven children).

My Grandma Bet was a big supporter of Barry Goldwater and was an alternative delegate at the Republican Convention in San Francisco in 1964, when Goldwater lost to Lyndon Johnson.

Her two children, my dad and Aunt Nancy, were, perhaps, even more conservative.

And, so, I was, too, for my boyhood years, attending rallies for Republican candidates, walking the precincts with my dad, poor-mouthing Democrats to my fellow elementary school friends.

I was in third grade when JFK was killed, and, sadly, because I grew up in a house where Kennedy was loathed, I honestly didn't feel too bad about his death, until I saw my stepmother crying, which sent all manner of weird signals to me. The man sounded so bad to my young and undiscerning ears that I figured, to use the legendary Texas defense, the man needed killin'.

Things changed quickly, though, in the late 1960s and into the 1970s. There was the Vietnam War, there was Woodstock and Kent State and Dylan and Nixon. I read more than once Hunter Thompson's still-brilliant *Fear and Loathing on the Campaign Trail '72*. I bought armloads of albums full of protest songs. I joined a rock-and-roll band. I grew my hair long.

And I literally gave my dad ulcers. He was in equal parts angry and grief-stricken by how I turned out. Especially the part about looking like a girl. He went to talk to the priest at our church.

"Does he do drugs? Has he been in jail? Are his grades good?"

I don't think that's what Dad wanted to hear. I think he wanted remedies. Deprogramming. God, please just give him a haircut!

So, big disappointment there. I don't tend to dabble in politics until I get angry enough to blast out a column, though I strive to maintain a humorous tone, nevertheless. Nobody wants to listen to some fat guy screaming in matters outside his expertise, unless that man is Rush Limbaugh.

I'm not including any of my political screeds here because they're fairly dated. There's no use dragging the NRA and Mitt Romney and all that back out into the light.

Once, though, I covered a presidential nominating convention. It wasn't one you've ever heard of.

WHERE'S THE PARTY?

Editor's note: Columnist Tim Grobaty dropped into the Reform Party Convention Thursday to try to sort out the confusing events. Here's his report:

The divisiveness among the warring factions of the Reform Party is killing us. Literally killing us. OK, not literally killing us, but making us sweat like a cold beer bottle dragged outside on a hot day.

And it's made our job, this divisiveness has, almost impossible.

Consider what, in a one-convention world, would have been a brisk exchange that we engineered between warring delegates from Arizona:

We're at the Long Beach Convention Center, where the Pat Buchanan faction of the Reform Party is meeting, and we're looking at these people who look comfortable in denim vests that proclaim Arizona the GRAND BUCHANAN STATE, curiously using the Grand Canyon, the very icon of schism-icity, to tout their man.

So, we hike what has to be half a mile, in heat that has to be 120 degrees, to the Terrace Theater, home of the splintering sect of the Reform Party, where we find Jim Bourassa, the founding chairman of the Reform Party in Arizona, who says, as a matter of fact, that he does "have a problem with how Buchanan has his own people who he's calling Reform Party delegates" and that the whole matter will be settled in court.

We trudge back down the stairs, past the fountain, down through the backlot of the Long Beach Arena, up Seaside Way, over to Pine Avenue, up the stairs, across the Promenade, and back into the Convention Center, where we find the denim-vest people and ask Their Leader if the name Jim Bourassa rings a bell.

"Yeah. I've seen him around."

"Well," we say, "he has a problem with you guys."

"Does he?" the denimmed delegate responds, in a manner that indicate he cares about as much about Bourassa's little "problem" as he does about what we had for lunch last Monday.

I continue, "Um. Yes, and—"

"I choose not to talk about it. Thank you for asking, though," he says.

We choose to end the conversation anyway, as the only fun we'd been having so far in this back-and-forth style of give-and-take is asking, "Where's the REAL convention?" of each candidate's spokespeople.

On one leg of our cross-convention travels, we run smack into Colonel Oscar Poole, an alternate delegate from the Great State of Georgia and proprietor of Poole's Bar-B-Q Pig Hill of Fame in East Ellijay, Georgia.

The Colonel (so called because he's "The Colonel Sanders of Barbecue") is decked out in a screamingly yellow blazer and an Uncle Sam top hat (plus, you know, some other clothes), and he proclaims the divisiveness is healthy for the entire world. "It's the American system at work," he says. "It's grassroots. It's giving the little man a voice. It's what the Reform Party is all about."

We note that, little man aside, how can the Reform Party run a country, when it can't get a handful of Arizonans to sit in the same room, and how the whole thing is sort of unrealistic, anyway, since even a unanimously nominated Reform Party candidate, at this point, would be trailing the dead thoroughbred racehorse Swaps by a length and a half in the polls.

The Colonel laughs and switches the subject to how Buchanan was out to his barbecue joint one time, and "I gave him a pig."

Our next stop is back inside the Convention Center, where we go shopping for souvenirs. But everything's so fanatical and dogmatic, and there's all these books and bumper stickers about how the country's going to hell, but maybe the Reform Party will bring it back to its once-glorious standing.

We finally settle on one of those stuffed birds—this one's a patriotic American eagle—that repeats everything you say, though it's mercifully turned off. The bird, however, is not for sale. Rather, it's being raffled off by the Greater Orange County Chapter of the Reform Party. We offer to buy the thing outright for $10.

"Nope. It's not for sale," says Marie Sayles.

"Twenty-five dollars," we counter.

"No."

"One hundred and fifty. No, FIVE HUNDRED dollars."

"No."

"I will give you twenty-five thousand dollars for the talking eagle."

Now she's laughing like it's some kind of joke. Like we don't need this bird. And, amazingly, she turns the whole transaction into a parable.

"Even for twenty-five thousand dollars, no, because we stick to our principles. We say something and our word is good."

On our way home, we run into You—yes, that's her full name—of Boulder, Colorado, who's standing out on Ocean Boulevard waving a Hagelin sign at traffic.

"How come no one's honking, You?" we ask, feeling just a tad irritated by her name, combined with the heat.

"I got a few honks earlier," she says, moving the sign around so rapidly no one could begin to read it.

You is in Hagelin's camp primarily because of his platform plank that urges labeling of genetically engineered food.

We talk for a bit as the traffic snakes by quietly. Then, a car full of Hagelinites pulls up to ask where's the cheapest parking.

"Honk your horn," we demand.

The Hagelin man pushes what should be the horn, but no sound comes out. He bashes at the wheel several times. Nothing.

"Crappy rental," he explains, and pulls out looking for a place to park at bargain rates so he can go in and listen to his man, the darker horse of the two-party Reform Party candidates, describe what America will be like when he becomes president.

When it comes to the more brutally divisive twenty-first century, with the ascendency of the Tea Party and a time when no one with any affiliation could be said to be behaving well, things changed in the public forum, and, let's face it, the Internet once again became part of the problem as it greedily wrenched just a little more from what used to belong in the realm of the newspaper: public bickering and reasoned argument.

And, once again, the Internet flew out of control without the careful filtering that opinion editors once provided, especially in the always-popular Letters to the Editor section.

The *Press-Telegram* used to receive dozens of these per day, with writers ranging from lunatics to well-educated professionals. The editors sawed off the peaks, tossing aside the profane rants along with the lengthy theses. It was a careful and balanced selection process, a far distant thing from what goes on in the raving-mad comments sections on blogs and news sites on the web.

Our genre of choice in writing about politics was satire. And we should tell you, in case you don't know: Satire doesn't work when you throw it out there in front of the thousands of varieties of readers with their varying intellects and levels of sweet naiveté.

WE'VE JOINED THE TEA PARTY. THAT'S HOW SORRY WE ARE

One of our Facebook friends—and was the term "friend" ever stretched so thin before Facebook?—has proclaimed that everyone who voted for Barack Obama owes America an apology.

We have grappled with Tea Party Republicans since the days when they called themselves "teabaggers," until some meddling know-it-all pointed them to Urban Dictionary.

And now, after much reflection, and more tequila

than you can carry in one trip, and a possible concussion, we are beginning to come around to the Tea Party's point of view.

For one thing, we, too, want our country back. We miss playing in the park without helicopter parents in those days before child molestation became all the rage in the Jimmy Carter administration. Plus, pollywogs. We want our pollywogs back.

But right now, we're apologizing to America for voting for Barack Obama. We are learning what a horrible, tragic mistake we made when we voted for him. Twice.

We are learning to dislike him in baby steps. We haven't got up to his swiping our guns or turning America into a Muslim state or something-something Benghazi. That's for the thetan-level Tea people.

Rather, our apologies stem from Obama's unforgivable day-to-day behavior.

We apologize for voting for a man who salutes with a cup of coffee in his hand. Short of making up a fraudulent war to send soldiers off to fight there is no greater or more cynical sign of disrespect to the U.S. military. Other than making them hold an umbrella over your head in the rain. That's the worst thing of all.

We apologize for voting for a man who has dandyish and foppish tastes in food. Obama made news (well, not real news, but news on the Anti-Obama Network) for expressing a preference for gherkin pickles in his egg salad. You couldn't make up a more la-dee-da ingredient. A dash of saffron, m'lord? Possibly, some more forgiving people might have let the gherkin thing slide as a one-off fetish acquired in Obama's Kenyan boyhood, but then your president let slip that he likes spicy mustard on his hamburgers, rather than yellow mustard. Well, excuse us, Your Royal Freakin' Highness. The Anti-Obama Network referred to Obama as the Poupon President. That was derision he had coming.

We apologize for voting for a man who plays golf too much. There are watchdogs out there who keep tabs on how much golf, or vacations in general, presidents enjoy, and there have been some who vacationed heartier than Obama, but none of the great ones ever picked up a club. Lincoln, Washington, Jefferson. Zero rounds of golf among them. A cursory glance at Web pages built by Tea-Partyists will show you that Obama has been golfing during every disaster of any size that has occurred in the U.S. since 2009.

We apologize for voting for a man who sometimes wears a tan suit. What, the tailor was all out of seer-sucker? Whattaya wear clown shoes in that kind of getup?

There's more. Oh, is there ever more! But we hope this will serve as adequate apology. Now, we've gotta go meet the gang and misspell some protest signs.

The following day, after that column, oddly, was greeted warmly by Conservatives and not so warmly by Liberals, we wrote this:

WELL, THAT WENT OVER WELL

Maybe we're not cut out for satire. Our Tuesday column, about how we have decided to join the Tea Party because Obama prefers spicy mustard on his hot dogs, occasionally wears a tan suit, saluted improperly one time, and a handful of other similarly grievous faults makes him utterly unable to run the United States. We apologized for ever having voted for him (an apology that was demanded by one ultraconservative on Facebook) and promised to dedicate our life to Teapartyism. Because we're a moron.

Reader Chris Richey saw this coming. "This is one of your best columns ever!" he wrote. "But I wonder if the point will get across to the people who need to 'get it'?"

Who knows? Let's find out.

"Welcome aboard!" chirped one caller on a phone message.

"Your apology is accepted. Good article," said a gracious reader.

"I really enjoyed it," said another. "I'm so glad you finally saw the light."

"Your article hit the spot," said one woman who we thought might have understood it. "You couldn't have written a better article regarding Obama," she continued. "Let's get him out. He will destroy the United States."

In a Letter to the Editor, Rosie Bauman of Lakewood wrote, "I am often not quite sure if Mr. Grobaty is joking or serious. Tuesday's column is a case in point.

"I sincerely hope that he is serious when he writes that he is apologizing for voting for Obama—TWICE!

"It takes a big man to admit when he is wrong, and yes, you were definitely wrong in voting for this arrogant, incompetent man."

How bad is Obama? Many groups in this paranoia-panicked neo-far right aren't bashful about calling him a terrorist, a fact not lost on reader Carol Smith, who, like some of us, including many Republicans, have just about had a bellyful of the Tea Party's gleeful ignorance.

"People can dislike the president," writes Smith. "Dislike his policies, think our country is totally on the wrong track, and believe that President Obama is a bad president, but how on Earth can that translate to 'terrorist'? Good Lord, whatever happened to reason in our country?"

TTIM FOR MITT

Finally, Election Day is here and once Florida disentangles itself from its Goldbergian/steampunk election machines and Ohio finishes fighting off all desperate attempts of voters to vote, we can find out which direction our country is going to take over the next four years.

We have been touting Barack Obama ever since he was a happy little community activist in Illinois, but the closer we've come to this day, the more heavy thinking we've done. And, let's face it, the highest-ups here have gently guided us toward the right (something about our bread being buttered on a certain side and that butter's relationship to the bleak job market for freshly fired journalists). So, in a grand example of our open-mindedness and willingness to consider all sides of an argument, we are endorsing Mitt Romney for president of your United States. And here are just twenty reasons why:

1. Turns out we have more money than we thought we had. A lot more. So we'll pay less tax under Romney. That will make us the happiest we've been in four years.

2. When we consider whether we're better off now than we were four years ago, the answer is no. When Obama took office we were only fifty-three. That was better than the fifty-seven we became during his time in office. Our hope for youth is rapidly dwindling. It's time for a change.

3. We look forward to the very wealthy paying less tax. More trickle-down riches for us!

4. We got hit really hard on the side of the head with a snow shovel.

5. While we like Obamacare, it was really Romney's idea. Let's have the man who invented compassion be in charge.

6. Obama isn't a big enough hero. He didn't kill Osama bin Laden. Navy SEALs did.

7. Obama is going to take all our guns and, possibly, Jesus.

8. Romney is better for the environment. He wanted

to let General Motors go bankrupt. Obama instead "rescued" General Motors and its smog-spewing, oil-quaffing products.

9. Obama got a fancy law degree from Harvard. Romney got one, too, but he didn't gild the lily by being president of the *Harvard Law Review*. That's just gaudy.

10. Mitt is a better and probably less-Muslimistical middle name than Hussein.

11. Romney was born in Michigan. There's absolutely no way of knowing for sure where Obama was born, but, in absence of an undoctored videotape of his exiting his mother's womb while holding a copy of that day's *Honolulu Advertiser,* we have to assume he was born in Kenya.

12. Romney has gallantly apologized for "making" his dog enjoy a fun and refreshing ride strapped to the roof of Romney's car. Obama has halfheartedly apologized for smoking dope in high school.

13. Obama wants to let the federal government continue to pay for Medicare, while Romney supports letting the elderly cut their own sweet deals in the lucrative private sector gold rush.

14. We have to admit we were largely swayed by bumper stickers such as "I'll keep my freedom, guns and money, you keep your CHANGE!" and "Somewhere in Kenya or Indonesia a village is missing its idiot." What really tipped us to the Romney side was "America or Obama. You can't

have both." That is so true, when you think about it. Especially after the snow-shovel incident.

15. Obama said we didn't start our small business all by ourselves, which really ticked us off, even though we've never had a small business. We do, however, write all by ourselves, with no government assistance other than all the things we're not thinking about because we're so puffed up with pride in the fact that we write all by ourselves.

16. Romney wants things to go back to the way they were (no specific date or era; just when we were very, very happy). Obama is still clinging to that tiresome "hope" thing and the "future" of America.

17. Obama plays a lot of basketball. Perhaps too much basketball. Romney was on the pep squad in prep school. We submit that this country needs pep more than a small forward.

18. Obama said he'd help New York and New Jersey after Hurricane Sandy. There's still water all over the place. Promise broken.

19. Paul Ryan wants to cut taxes for the very wealthy, end Medicare, give more tax breaks to big oil, slash education budgets, decimate Social Security, and slay Big Bird. Joe Biden laughed at him during the debates. There's no excuse for bad behavior. Point: Ryan.

20. We're getting tired of blaming Bush for everything. With Romney as president, we won't have to do that anymore.

(AFTERWARD) WE WERE BEING SARCASTIC!

Wow. We wrapped up our yearlong presidential election coverage on Tuesday with a column about how we were all of a sudden backing Mitt Romney, and the response was breathtaking in its scope of how it was deciphered by some of our more credulous but cherished readers. God bless you all, and God bless America.

Sarcasm is a fragile thing, and our attempt at the ethereal form was stomped on like a groom's glass at a Jewish wedding by some readers.

We thought that Reason No. 4 for why we switched to Romney, "We got hit really hard on the side of the head with a snow shovel," would introduce enough slapstick to give a hint that we were sort of tongue-in-cheeking the thing, but apparently we needed more warning stickers.

A few Romney Republicans thanked us and the newspaper for backing their man. And some Obama Democrats excoriated us for single-handedly sabotaging their man's effort. One such fellow suggested we'd be comfortable wearing a white sheet for some reason.

In a Letter to the Editor, David Freeman of Long Beach wrote, "There may be good reasons to vote for Romney as he is a decent man, but this list is mostly lies. Appears Grobaty did learn the GOP way of just LIE and our feeble-minded public might be swayed."

Sigh. Somebody hand us a snow shovel.

As for church, Christ, I don't know. The drift away from the Holy Mother could've come from the mild torture of all those dark recitations of the rosary or from the terrifying nuns in Catholic school with their towering wimples and dark, flowing robes, or the way-not-brief-enough time at an all-boys Catholic school before I tunneled out of there and into the loving embrace of public school at Wilson High. However it came to be, the departure from Catholicism was slower, though just as inevitable, than my escape from Conservatism. I stopped going to Mass sometime around high school, telling my folks I was going to church and then driving off to the park to sit in the shade and read for an hour.

In later years I drifted along toward Catholic agnosticism and finally to Catholic atheism. Still a Catholic, though, just without the beliefs.

Once, while interviewing humorist P. J. O'Rourke, as I slipped into a haze of Heinekens at the Beverly Wilshire Hotel, the humorist/author confessed that Catholics are funnier than people brought up in any other religion (he was brought up Episcopalian, like there's a difference). Second, of course, are Jews. After that, it's an ecumenical tie for a distant third. Lutherans aren't in the hunt.

I still often think like a Catholic, and the Catholic God and I have a cordial relationship—a little too cordial for some of my readers who howl sacrilege when I dabble with the subject. But, for me, God is one of my favorite topics.

BUSTING INTO CHURCH

Our Lutheran friend Jerry Lossner, pastor of St. Philip Lutheran Church in Compton, annually tests the limits of our friendship by insisting that we do more articles on the Baby Jesus every December.

And now in a note he writes, "My good friend Rick Kemppainen, superintendent of the Bellflower Unified School District, is a member of my former church in Bellflower, and he, too, thinks your Christmas articles need more emphasis on Christ."

What is this, a democracy all of a sudden? It's a slippery slope, opening ourselves up to requests. We give in on the Christ Issue and how long will it be before people start sending up cocktail napkins on which is scrawled, "Now do a column with a Chihuahua, a giant cigar, and a Frenchman in it."

But, OK, here we go: Here's one about Christ—and Pastor Lossner will be delighted that it's the Lutheran version, not the Catholic version, although, after further thought, it probably is about the Catholic version of God, who interceded for us at a Lutheran church about eighteen years ago. And by "interceded" we mean "helped us break into."

It was a Friday in late December, and we were picking up our two-year-old son, Ray Charles, from day care at a Lutheran Church, because at that time Catholics didn't offer day care because Catholic women were supposed to stay home having babies at a Mormon clip, so we went to the Lutheran place because it was close to our mother-in-law's home and adjacent to a fine coffee house. Throw in a bar and a Mexican restaurant, and we would've left Ray there eighteen hours a day.

Anyhow, on this one Friday, just before the center was to close for a week for Christmas, there was a note on the bulletin board that the kids had been exposed to such-and-such a dreadful and contagious illness, and there was a list of symptoms attached, which we didn't bother to read because who has all day to stand around reading bulletin boards, am I right, boys?

TURNS OUT WE SHOULD'VE READ IT: So, on Saturday afternoon, Ray gets real sick, and we're starting to wonder if it's that such-and-such a disease and we're wishing we had looked at the symptoms, because if he has it, it could be a bad, bad thing, so we motor across town to see if we can get into the day-care center to look at the bulletin board, but we can't. Everyone's gone, and everything's locked up. *Whatever happened to trust?* we wonder sadly.

So we go all around the perimeter, trying windows and seeing if maybe we can't BREAK INTO A CHURCH, but nothing's opened or unlocked. Except the main front door that was not quite shut. This is the part where we credit our Catholic God, because we can't imagine a Lutheran God helping us bust into His own church. That's just Theology 101.

So, now we're in the nave, the main part, where you would sit if you were Lutheran, and we look around to see if there's anything worth stealing. Our

God goes, "Stealing? You're going to steal from a church? I raised you better than that."

We assured Him we were kidding (still looking around, though, to see if there was a guitar somewhere; Christians play nice guitars. Badly, generally, but still . . .), and we started looking for a way to get from the church to the day-care center, and, after a bit, we found it: through a door that led to a courtyard. We opened the door and stepped into the courtyard and, like in a stupid movie, it slammed shut, locked, behind us.

"Come on!" we said to the air around us. "We weren't going to take a guitar even if there had been one."

But there we were, locked out of everything, so thoroughly away from the outside that we couldn't even yell, "Help! We've broken into a church!"

GETTING IN: All the windows and doors are closed in the courtyard. Except one. There's your God again: "(He Always Leaves) One Window Open" should be the name of a hymn.

It's the window that leads into the infants' room, and we kinda fall into a crib as we flop through the open window. We squall a bit in pain as we make our way into the hallway and read the bulletin board. Turns out Ray doesn't have any of the dire symptoms. He probably has a cold.

We still have to get out of the place, which is fairly difficult and involved us clambering up to the roof by climbing a tree and then jumping down 12 feet to our death, or, rather, sweet, sweet freedom.

And we all agreed, it was the best Christmas ever, because we finally found the true meaning of the holiday.

We enjoyed a nice eggnog laced with whiskey, brandy, and rum and toasted our God who helped us break into, and get out of, a Lutheran church.

JESUS'S WIFE

A historian of early Christianity at Harvard Divinity School has identified a scrap of papyrus that she says was written in Coptic in the fourth century and contains a phrase never seen in any piece of Scripture: "Jesus said to them, 'My wife . . . '")

"Honey, I'm home!" yells Jesus just before he takes a header over the ottoman. His briefcase bursts open and papyrus leaves litter the living room floor.

Jesus's wife comes into the living room from the kitchen. She's wearing a frilly apron and she's covered with flour. "Are you OK?" she asks.

"I'm fine," says Jesus, getting to his feet and picking up the papers. "I don't know why you keep rearranging the furniture." He notices his wife's appearance. "What's with the flour?"

"I've been making loaves all day for the fish barbecue tonight," said Jesus's wife.

"I've told you before," said Jesus. "I only need a couple of loaves and a few fish. It'll be plenty for everyone. You're just throwing money away."

Jesus's wife pouts and starts to cry.

"Oh, honey, I'm sorry," says Jesus. A bouquet of roses suddenly appears in Jesus's wife's arms. "Flowers are your answer for everything," she scowls. The roses turn into a basket of dinosaur puppies, to Jesus's wife's delight.

"How was your day?" asks the placated wife of Jesus.

"Busy. Helped Pop at the shop for a while, chased some guys selling bootleg T-shirts in the Temple. Wrote a speech for that thing on the Mount I have to do next week. I hate public speaking. Dad was better at it."

"No, sweetie," said Jesus's wife. "You're much better than your dad. He just bellowed at everyone. I don't think he knows how much he frightens people when he talks."

"You're an angel," said Jesus. "You think I have time to relax before the fellas come over?"

"They're not due for an hour yet," said Jesus's wife. "Why don't you take a dip in the pool?"

"Can't," said Jesus. "I keep bouncing off the water when I try to jump in."

Jesus settles into a Barcalounger while his wife goes into the kitchen to chop celery.

"Who all's coming?" she shouts over her shoulder.

"Most of the guys, though Thomas is doubtful," Jesus replies.

"I swear to God, I'll never get tired of that joke," yelps Jesus's wife, starting in on the onions.

Peter and Paul arrive together as always. Jesus's wife gives them both big *mmwah* air kisses and accepts the two jugs of water they hand her.

"What's this?" says Jesus's wife, though clearly it's water.

"It's wine," says Paul.

"Really?" says Jesus's wife. "You're going to make Jesus do the water-into-wine thing?"

"Wine not?" jokes Peter the punster. "And ask him to make this one a nice Northern Rhône–style Syrah, if he can swing it."

"You guys are unbelievable," says Jesus's wife.

Jesus is out by the pool grilling cod and wearing his "Kiss Me, I'm Nazarene" apron when Luke and Judas show up with their dates. Jesus gives Luke a big hug. "My man!" he says. He nods, barely cordially, at Judas. "Jude," he says coolly.

Jesus's wife comes out with a platter of deviled eggs. "How many more followers do you have, Jesus?"

"To everyone who knocks, the door will be opened," replies Jesus.

"I wrote that," says Luke. "Luke 11:10. Look it up."

"You wrote what I said," counters Jesus.

"*Potato, patato,*" says Jesus's wife.

"Nobody says *patato,*" says Simon, wandering in with a couple of loaves.

"What is it with all the loaves?" asks Jesus. "I only need two or three."

"You needed five the first time, honey," Jesus's wife reminds him. "You needed seven the second time."

"I wrote about it," said Mark. "It was the fish you needed only two of."

"Everybody committed the cardinal sin of filling up on bread," recalls Matthew.

"Technically, that's not a cardinal sin," says Jesus.

"Aaaanyway . . ." says an exasperated Jesus's wife.

Hours later, after everyone has gone home, Jesus is hosing off the patio while Jesus's wife gathers up the cocktail glasses.

"All those guys, Matthew, Mark, Luke, and John always write about you. How come they never mention me?"

"You're implied in everything I do," says Jesus. "Behind every great man is a great woman."

"You're being condescending," whines Jesus's wife, who is suddenly holding a basket of dinosaur kittens.

"I don't want any kittens!" screams Jesus's wife. "I just want someone to mention that you're not doing all this yourself! I do half the work around here!"

"OK," says Jesus. "I'll have someone write a little something in the morning. It's too late to make it in the book, but we'll get it out eventually."

With that, he walks across the pool and turns off the halogen lights, then he comes back and takes his wife's hand and Jesus and Jesus's wife hit the hay.

_____

CHAPTER SIXTEEN

Puppies as Panacea

If you're going to monkey around with politics and religion, you need to have a kennel full of puppies to keep yourself employed. You unleash controversial subjects when you want to rile up the readership, something that's encouraged by columnists' bosses. It is certainly not difficult to rile people up. If it is your desire to have a lot of people yelling, "Asshole!" at you, all you need to do is bring up your politics and mock-patiently explain the "facts" of your unassailable position regarding candidates and issues. It's bracing.

Then, just about when your readers are ready to explode or cancel their subscriptions, you release the hounds and next thing you know they're eating out of your hands like a baby llama at a petting zoo.

I could do a whole book just on my dog, Jimmy, and God knows, there's money in dog books. In fact, we could put out a whole book on Jimmy's most quotable lines because, yes, he could talk. A non-talking dog doesn't do a columnist any good. It's like a gun-shy dog for a hunter. You just give him to the nice couple down the street. Rather than an entire book, here are just a couple. You want more? Buy our next book.

A LOT OF MONEY
FOR A LITTLE DEWCLAW

We are rapidly running out of money, because we own a dog. And don't start in on us, buster, about the terminology. We own this dog. You want to quibble over that, you pay the vet bills, which, due to Jimmy's latest little prank, are rapidly closing in on the $1,000 mark.

Now, $1,000 used to buy you a lot of dog. For $1,000 you could get a dog who would do things like tell us if our daughter, Hannah, was stuck in a well or get beers out of the fridge or at least catch a Frisbee. Or fetch a stinkin' tennis ball. Jimmy does none of those things, and much, much more.

Here's what happened to our idiot dog, that we own. We were going to a Cinco de Mayo party with our longtime friends and neighbors, the Cop Across the Street Family. Jimmy really, really likes the Cop Family, chiefly because Mrs. Cop always throws chunks of steer at him, so he started screaming like a girl when he saw us all walking down the street toward the Cinco bash, leaving him at the house.

Next thing you know, he's rocketing down the street after us. Turns out he had jumped out our son's window but, because he's overweight by roughly a picnic ham, he failed at his first attempt, apparently, ripping off, practically, his right front dewclaw.

As far as we know, there is no more useless part of any animal than a dewclaw. Our dictionary actually uses the word "functionless" in describing the little pad about a third of the way up his leg. So we figured fixing up the thing, either by lopping it off altogether or sewing it back on—hey, you're the vet, you figure it out—would cost, at the absolutely most outrageous, $65. That was the number in our head.

No. Our wife took Jimmy to the emergency animal hospital, and there went $187 just to bandage him up and wait for something like the Dewclaw Reattachment Crisis Team to be choppered in the next day, when Jimmy went in for surgery, which included things like $49.82 for pre-anesthesia, then $117.98 for the actual anesthesia, and on and on ($3.50 for "Biohazard Waste/Mgt—Out") to the tune of $603.10. For a torn dewdamclaw. And more bills loom, with the removal of stitches and follow-up visits.

A few years ago, a poodle belonging to one of our beloved editors was hit by a bus—A BUS!—and the bill was $600. That's OK. You get hit by a bus, and $600 doesn't seem that unfair.

Getting hit by a bus is a major moment in anyone's life. After that, all events are before-bus and after-bus. Getting a dewclaw lacerated, however, is a mere irritation. Jimmy will forget all about it by the time he eats another horsefly off the living room picture windowsill. We, on the other hand, will be paying for it for months, and even then, we still won't have a dog that can catch a Frisbee.

DOGGEDLY DISGRUNTLED

Jimmy loped into the Barn Tuesday night growling and wearing a disgruntled look on his face.

"What's up?" we asked, not really caring about the answer. Jimmy's disgruntlement usually has to do with someone walking past the house. For some reason, he really hates people using the sidewalk anywhere near our property.

Anyhow, he goes, "An idiot beagle won the Westminster Kennel Club Dog Show."

Jimmy and we don't see eye to eye on everything. We have a higher tolerance for UPS drivers, for one thing. We felt somewhat in favor of the beagle, if only for its underdog role. He was the New York Giants to a pair of poodles' Patriots.

We knew that the beagle, a cute little three-year-old named Uno—the first of its breed to win at Westminster in the 100 years that the club has presented a Best in Show award—was a crowd favorite, and we knew that Jimmy's breed mate, an Australian shepherd named Deuce, was among the finalists for Best in Show at Westminster. Nothing good was going to come of this in the Hot! household.

"It was time for a beagle to win," we said, trying

to bring some fifties-style sitcom-dad reason to the argument.

"You love beagles so much, why didn't you get one?" snapped Jimmy.

"You were free," we said. "Beagles cost money."

"There are plenty of other differences," barked James, trotting over to the intricate jumble of tubes that is the Internet and calling up the Iams breed comparison feature at iams.com.

"Look," he yapped. "Aussie: 'Not much barking.' Beagle: 'Likes baying.'"

Jimmy continued, checking the comparison chart: "Aussies, it says, are 'moderately protective.' Your beagle, though, 'Loves everyone.'"

"Check one in the beagle's column," we said.

"Discernment is a good thing," argued Jim. "Get a beagle and pretty soon the UPS guy is marching off with your stereo and stemware."

"An Australian shepherd, it says, is 'fairly independent,' while a beagle is 'moderately dependent on poodles,'" continued Jimmy, reading from the screen.

"That's 'people.' Moderately dependent on 'people,' not 'poodles,'" we said. "Who taught you how to read?"

"Look, go down the list," said Jimmy. "Guarding? Aussie, yes; beagle, no. Herding? Aussie, yes; beagle, no. Search and rescue? Aussie, yes; beagle, no."

"Look here," we said. "Hunting? Aussie, no; beagle, yes."

"The list is flawed! My mom killed a giant killer deer in Ohio with her bare hands," said Jimmy. It's a story that Jimmy never gets tired of telling, and he bristles at anyone who falls into the camp of those who say Jimmy's mother may have just found a dead deer and decided to drag it home to our cousin's farm to snack on it at her leisure. And it might have been a little fawn in any case, not an elk or a moose or a dragon—all variations that Jimmy has used in telling the story.

Westminster judges weren't in the business of comparing breeds for ownership purposes, and if they are at all swayed by audience reaction, they did the right thing in giving Uno the top-dog honors.

The little tri-colored yapper won in the hounds category in December's AKC/Eukanuba show in Long Beach. The Long Beach overall winner, Charmin, a Sealyham terrier, won in its group at Westminster but, like the four-year-old Aussie Deuce, lost to the clearly overjoyed beagle who frolicked and bayed in front of the cameras and crowds.

"Yeah, all very impressive," said Jimmy in his smuggest possible voice. "But let me ask you this: Can this Uno dog carry on a conversation?"

"Nope," we said, flipping the channel on the TV over to Animal Planet's *Orangutan Island.* "But the ability to talk is not exactly a selling point in a dog, especially when you won't do it in front of anyone else. Like that time on David Letterman when you sat there."

Our dog hasn't spoken to us since.

JIMMY GROBATY, 1998–2013

We had our handsome Australian shepherd Jimmy put down Saturday morning.

If we were a hero, we would've done it months ago, by which time he'd already gone mostly blind, mostly deaf (though he could still hear the kibble hitting his dog dish), and mostly unable to walk.

At dawn Saturday, Jimmy was finished, so we scooped him up and took him for the last of a thousand car rides to the vet's, where he was dispatched to, as those of us who have had dogs have always desperately wished, Dog Heaven (sometimes called Cat Hell).

We introduced Jimmy to readers on October 6, 1998, with the opening line of our column: "We got a dog." And we unabashedly admitted that while it was ostensibly for the benefit of our young children, "We really got him because we figured he would make great column fodder and we would never have to work very hard again."

It worked like a dream. Jimmy romped his way through scores of our columns over his fifteen years. He even talked sometimes, which was pretty off-putting. Talking dogs aren't as amusing as you'd imagine.

When he was three, we ran a picture of Jimmy standing in a water fountain at a public school, drinking out of one of the spigots. Something he used to do all the time. The photo tore the city apart. There was outrage from half the city calling it "gross," "disgusting," and "sick," while more reasoned responders came to his defense.

"With germs that you'll find at a public school, your dog is lucky to be alive," wrote one. "I went to school with my kid one time and I was out for two weeks."

Jimmy always wanted to be with us, especially when we went to his favorite place, the Cop Across the Street's house. The Cop Across the Street had the ironic initials CATS. Nothing we could do would prevent Jimmy from coming over. He'd always find some escape route even if it meant just crashing *Die Hard*–style through a closed window, which he did one Cinco de Mayo, resulting in the expensive removal of a torn-up dewclaw.

Although Jimmy wasn't wild about trips to the vet, he sure managed a lot of ways to get there. His monthly medical expenditures prompted more fodder: "If you're in a hurry to get rid of a lot of money, your best bet is to get a dog," we wrote in 2009, when he incurred more than $2,000 in bills. "If you're allergic to dogs, then you've gotta do something else to get rid of that much money in a rush: Buy a new Jaguar off the showroom floor and take it out and drive it into a tree."

Whenever we went on vacation, Jimmy was put in the protective care of the Cop Across the Street, which invariably led to disaster. "To Protect and Serve" is apparently just a decal cops slap on their cars.

At least two entire columns were given to the Cop losing Jimmy, resulting in sweeping neighborhood dog hunts.

"The exact story remains fuzzy thanks to conflicting narratives," we wrote about one escape. "But it involves people throwing shoes and strangers emerging glassy-eyed and shouting and all manner of he-went-thataways . . . "

And we wrote, maybe too often, about Jimmy's ineptitude.

"Can't catch a novelty flying disc, can't retrieve a tennis ball ('Can't or won't?' he once said in his own defense), can't walk in a straight line, can't not mess up the house, and is about as obedient as a Greenpeace protester." How do you miss a dog like that? Badly. We miss him badly.

CHAPTER SEVENTEEN

Who Died and Made Me a Columnist?

Here's a question for me: Who died and made me a columnist? It's a good question, because being a columnist has always been a pretty big deal in journalism. A columnist is the only writer on a newspaper who is allowed, encouraged even, to bloviate on any topic at hand. Of course, everyone has an opinion, so why does it matter what a columnist thinks any more than, say, your guy on a barstool (there is a frequent overlap there, by the way)?

A columnist gets weight added to his words with the credibility and weaponry of the newspaper behind him. The columnist has, ideally, been trained in journalism, working his way up, in my case, from the bottom. He has covered cops, politics, church carnivals, funerals, 100-year-olds' birthdays, the weather, disasters, and elections (a little more overlap). He's interviewed survivors, widows and widowers, the tiresome man on the street, the winners of poetry contests, movie stars, murderers, scientists, and CEOs. He's stuck his nose in every part of the city he's lived in until, finally, he gets to air his opinions and thoughts in the newspaper of record.

He's seen dead people.

And, yes, somebody has to die, or at least finally retire, for him to become a columnist, because columnists don't happily relinquish their crowns.

And retirement is hard on them. Almost invariably they try to hang on to their status after quitting the job, arranging to write a weekly column from their vacation spots and retirement houses. It never works, and they just fade away to nothing. It's sad, really. The graceful departure is either to just stop writing for the paper or keel over in the newsroom, a valorous act that adds a couple of decades to your legacy.

I'm in an odd position for a columnist, by being one of the few who is engaged in the race to the grave with the newspaper itself. It's neck and neck as I write this. The paper is losing a subscriber with the death of every elderly reader in town, and young people aren't standing in line waiting to inherit the subscription.

And, if you want to know the truth, I don't feel so hot myself.

FOR OUR BIRTHDAY:
WARM BLANKETS AND OPIATES

You will certainly recall our uneventful visit to the doctor last September when he told us we were at the age where our body was going to be falling apart soon.

We got to that age Monday. We woke up around 2 a.m. Monday, at the age of sixty years and two hours, with a pain on the left side of our abdomen. It wasn't your typical pain. This was the kind of pain that spurred ancient civilizations to build temples and pyramids in an attempt to appease the gods in hopes that they would dial things back to simple famine and sundry plagues.

We had laughed at the doctor's dire bedside-mannerless prophecy. Surely, we'd get a little grace period after getting to "that age." A sort of easing-in process with a few niggling woes marking the early innings; a cold, tear-duct malfunction, liver spots, slow healing of scratches on the arm. Certainly not the sort of pain that caused us to run out into the yard and roll around in the dirt, howling pitifully, wide-eyed and slobbering and wondering what kind of horrors would be visited upon us at sixty-one.

Eventually it dawned on us that we're not a hero. We weren't going to be able to man up and walk it off. We stumbled into the bedroom where our wife was snoozing peacefully and dreaming about chasing bunnies in a meadow until our animal shrieking woke her up.

She drove us to Community while we groaned and wept and swore in three languages.

The second we hit the hospital bed in emergency we felt a lot better. The pain had receded to kind of like how you'd feel if you got hit by a skip loader.

We were wheeled in our bed down several long hallways and a couple of different floors to get a CAT scan. If we were incredibly wealthy, this would be the only way we'd go anywhere. It was all we could do to not yell, "Wheeee!" as we lay on a pile of pillows under a blanket that had just come out of a blanket-toaster. We've stayed in some world-class hotels in our life, but this was the swankiest of them all. Most hotels, they make you walk from place to place.

Also, we didn't have to go through all the hassle of drinking water out of a glass like a poor person. Here, they just shoot it right into your veins.

The doctors eventually determined that we have kidney stones, which was a disappointment because kidney stones, like the other stupid ailment we have, trigger finger—in which our right ring finger locks up and has to be forced open—doesn't have the gravitas of your more esoteric maladies.

We were hoping for diverticu-something, which, just between you and us, we still think it might be, especially after talking to people who have had a) kidney stones and, b) diverticulitis.

Either, way, veterans of both cheerfully recall being in a staggering amount of pain.

And women who have had a. or b. are fairly unanimous in declaring the pain of either/both makes childbirth feel like you're being tickled with a little yellow feather.

For now, we're standing by, with our little container of Norco. That's another thing: At hotels they give you mints on your pillow. At Community, you get opiates.

Wheeeee!

COLONOSCOPY: A FUN MIX OF BELLAGIO AND LEGOLAND

With Valentine's Day just around the corner, we've been getting a lot of questions about our colonoscopy that we enjoyed on a sunny morning last week.

"What was the worst part, the procedure itself or the day before?" asked a friend who's been warily toying with the idea of getting one.

We'll tell you the worst part. The worst part is when you're lying on a bed in the clinic, wearing nothing but a flimsy backless gown and about fifteen minutes from getting a high-tech garden hose/flashlight/videocam shoved through your servants' entrance and one of the attendants says, "Hey, you're the guy who writes the column in the paper!" and then another nurse goes, "Yeah! I thought you looked familiar!" and another one says, "Oh, you're the person who wrote that? One of the doctors brought your colonoscopy column in last week."

We're pretty sure there's a photo on Facebook with the three of them posing and smiling with the subject at hand. That's how we squandered our fifteen minutes of fame.

Otherwise, sure, the day before was a lot worse than the day of. For one thing, we had to fast for a good twenty-four hours, which, in our case, was pretty doable. The bad part, as everyone knows—and what keeps people from getting a colonoscopy—is the "cleansing." And even that wasn't quite as bad as we had imagined. We're a great worst-case guy and the cleansing certainly didn't meet our lofty expectations of horror. Basically, it's just drinking 16 ounces of a solution, followed by 32 more ounces of water, and then the fun begins!

First, clear a wide and short path to the bathroom, and in a few minutes you're a human upside-down Bellagio water show for a couple of hours. You grab some sleep and then get up before dawn and do it again. By that point, your colon is clean enough to wear to the prom.

Barring being recognized by nurses and attendants (they recognized us by our face, in case you were wondering), the procedure itself was, for us anyway, more fun than Legoland.

Here's what happens: They stick a needle in your arm and hook you up to a bag of some sort of solution.

Then you're done.

Presumably, some guy is rattling around in your basement for thirty minutes, but you're blissfully dreaming of chasing butterflies in a meadow. We would totally do it again, except next time we'll do it in Albuquerque or somewhere else where we're not likely to be recognized.

A few months later, I was sitting around gabbing in the newsroom. There is no better place to gab than in the newsroom, because some of the brightest people I know are there. I'm not saying it's packed with bright people. You need a few boring people with no range to their knowledge to remind you that the whole world isn't choked with intelligence.

On any day, at any moment in a newsroom, you can hear reporters interviewing people on the phone. One is talking to a state senator about a bill that's been introduced to regulate truck exhaust around the port and harbor, while another is talking to the mother of a kid killed in a gang shooting, and another is talking to an attorney who is representing a group of seniors filing a class-action suit against an assisted living center.

The very next day, these same three reporters will be researching stories on what's killing the sea lions off the coast, the antics of a certain trustee on a university board, and the fight at the transit company about kickbacks from a bus manufacturer.

So I'm gabbing for a while with a couple of these people and I turn around to go back to writing and my entire right side has shut down.

It's not an unpleasant feeling, going all warmly numb and utterly inefficient on an entire side of your body, but it's off-putting because you know that's not how the body works when it's in top, or toppish, form. I've done stories about strokes. It's just another of those things I've been a brief expert on.

Things get a little meta here, because on this day, I was near the end of writing this book, and no one wants to die while writing a book humorously titled *I'm Dyin' Here*. An ironic death is a drag; it's the only thing people will talk about at your wake.

DON'T WORRY ABOUT US (SNIFF). WE'LL BE FINE

For maximum pity points, we have been telling people we had a stroke a couple of weeks ago. Not a full-on stroke, we've had to sadly admit. Rather, "sort of a series of strokey things," we've said, trying to keep "stroke" in the vocabulary of the conversation.

"Nothing to worry about," we've been saying with mock-valor, with just enough quiver in our voice to insure that people won't not worry.

What we in fact experienced was nothing more than a TIA, which is how Spanish-speakers yell the word "aunt" and what presumptive people use to shorten the term "thanks in advance." In the medical community, where there are no short words, TIA is a transient ischemic attack, which sounds a little bit like being assaulted by a school of hobo fish, which would make a great story to explain why we missed a few columns.

A TIA occurs when blood flow to a part of the brain is blocked by a clot for a short time before the symptoms go away, as opposed to a stroke, in which the blood flow stays blocked and there is permanent damage done to the brain. We didn't have that. Our brain is great. We have the brain of a healthy four-year-old.

We were at work (when are we ever not?) when the right side of our body went numb and our hand refused to do what it was told.

"I think I'm having a stroke," we said, which was met with gales of laughter, as is everything the office clown says. So we sat there looking stroke-like until Melissa Evans, our willowy city editor, took us to the emergency room at Community Hospital where, once it was discovered we had a splendid insurance plan, we were put through more tests than an astronaut: two CT scans, an MRI, echocardiogram, not to mention a bevy of blood tests and an enjoyable game of patty-cake with a neurologist. We could ace the LSAT now.

Specialists from every field came by our room like the however-many magi, bearing gifts of heart monitors, decidedly non-recreational drugs, and dire statistics about how frequently people who have had TIA go on to The Show with major-league strokes, which is the kind of thing that takes the cut out of your crease.

We spent a sleepless night in the hospital's heart center listening to someone's TV all night until we learned the exact cadence of sitcoms and the predictable occurrences and levels of canned laughter, while trying to figure out what the Sam Hill was going on out in the hall with various patients making unreasonable demands. And we learned that walking around in a backless gown while wheeling an IV holder adds a minimum of fifteen years to one's appearance.

The doctors at the hospital wanted to keep us another night, such are our charms and primo insurance, but we bolted out of there with nothing but the clothes on our back and a heart monitor that we have to wear for a month. It's like living with an amorous octopus.

And then off to San Clemente for a lot of rest and wrapping up the third draft of our book, *I'm Dyin' Here,* which title's irony continues to grow more ham-handed with each hospitalization.

CHAPTER EIGHTEEN

The Fall

Newspapers used to make people wealthy. Reporters could buy houses, editors could buy nice houses, columnists could buy a nice house and still have money left over for a Ping-Pong table and a week somewhere at an Embassy Suites for vacation. Publishers lived in mansions.

They didn't do it on readers' dimes (I know "dimes" is an outdated reference, but let's just let it stand as a sort of Forever Stamp for whatever you now need to dump into a newsrack). Papers were virtually given away so publishers could boast big circulation numbers, which in turn commanded higher prices for display advertisements and increase the effectiveness of classified ads.

Classifieds were those tiny ads that were in the last section of the paper. Tiny ads that were huge. The classifieds were America's marketplace: Homes for sale, apartments for rent, used cars, guitars, pianos, clock radios, gently used sofas and sectionals, appliances, lawnmowers, jobs wanted, employees sought, dogs lost, cats found. Love notes could be found in the classifieds, people looking for a second chance in missed connections. There was page after page after page of classifieds. They were what gave the newspaper the weight to be thrown from kids on bikes to subscribers' rooftops.

The splashier ads brought in some good money in big chunks, but nothing like the stacks of one-dollar bills the classifieds brought in. Those were the ads that paid for reporters and editors. The classifieds kept our sports reporters on the road, sent travel writers to faraway countries, bought extravagant gear for photographers and memberships at golf clubs like St. Andrews in Scotland and Cypress Point in Monterey for the publishers.

In short, classifieds counted for well more than 50 percent, sometimes as much as 70 percent, of a daily newspaper's revenue.

At the turn of the millennium, Craigslist fired up its free-advertising engine, but you couldn't hear it over the roar of the higher-ups, who I like to imagine tearing into grilled capons and boar and swilling ale and mead from massive flagons while wenches peeled grapes and sprawled on the conference tabletop.

Were the bosses scared? No. They were amused. These were businessmen, successful ones. They were on boards, commissions. They built buildings. They crowned kings in city government. And the first thing they learned in business school is that you don't get rich giving things away when you can sell them instead.

They laughed at Craigslist. How, they just barely wondered, is a company going to make any money by giving away free ads?

A better question would be why would anyone buy an ad when they can get one for free on Craigslist?

Craigslist took off and soared at roughly and not coincidentally at the same velocity that newspapers plummeted. It was the kind of g-force that makes you look like you stuffed a dinner plate in your mouth horizontally.

A study by researchers at business schools at USC and New York University reckoned that Craigslist resulted in a $5.4 billion loss in newspaper revenues between 2000 and 2007. And those, we would later recall, were the easy years.

Oh, and that wasn't all. We maybe could've grappled with Craigslist, but here's what else happened at roughly the same time: the cost of newsprint skyrocketed with a gleeful, suddenly capitalist China paying top dollar for it. In Asia, newspapers were growing, while in the United States, they were disappearing like wagons after the invention of the automobile. The economy was tanking ferociously, making those advertisers who had still been faithful to newspapers less anxious to buy ads in what became increasingly vain attempts to lure cash-strapped customers.

Joining classifieds in the exodus out of newspapers were automotive ads. Now dealers could show up-to-the-minute inventory online; supermarket ads, which had made Thursdays the most profitable day after Sunday in the newspaper industry with page upon page of grocery store ads, went with direct mail, choking your mailbox with glossy flyers and coupons. Remember theater ads? It was where people looked to see what was playing where and at what times. Theater chains stopped doing that. Again, why pay a newspaper for what they could get free on the Internet. That's all on your mobile device now, as is the ability to purchase tickets for the show. And how the flick in question is scoring on Rotten Tomatoes.

Subscription and rack rates went up to help take up the slack, which resulted in further loss of subscribers, which resulted in fewer people reading the paper, which resulted in reduced costs for advertisers who were rapidly losing interest anyway.

Competing with journalists were news aggregators, online news "papers," search engines that could point readers in precisely the direction they wanted to go without a team of editors deciding what they should be reading each morning. And millions and millions of bloggers, many of them little more than loudmouths with a laptop.

Throughout all this upheaval, journalists became jobless. More than 20 percent of them nationwide lost their jobs in the first part of the new century as papers slashed staff, if they didn't just go belly-up altogether.

Everywhere, in all major cities, newspapers disappeared or trimmed back to six or five or three days a week.

I started seeing myself as a neon-orange-dyed duck during duck-hunting season. Green-visored newspaper accountants trimmed the easy stuff. Did the *New York Times* really need a beer writer, a wine writer, *and* a spirits writer? Couldn't they find just one guy who would drink everything?

We'd had guys who just wrote about horseracing, who just wrote about hunting. Out went travel editors, society editors, radio critics, opera critics, dance critics. I had to wonder at what point a columnist would be considered a luxury or superfluous.

And that was the easy first wave of journalists. Next came the harder stuff. When the *Press-Telegram* was sold, it was made part of a chain of nine papers in Southern California, each of which had its own staff of writers, photographers, and editors. Each had its pro and college sports reporters, its political writers, its editorialists.

If you owned nine newspapers in one area, you might wonder if you also needed nine Dodger reporters. You didn't, as it turns out.

The newspaper became centralized. The *Press-*

Telegram's thundering presses were quieted as the printing took place somewhere I've never been. Gone, too, were all the pre- and post-production people. Linotype operators, engravers, mailers, truck drivers, printers, and pressmen. Circulation, too, was centralized. I don't know where all that happens now, either.

By 2010, the *Press-Telegram* had moved from its glorious four-story building at Sixth and Pine to a few floors of a beautiful fourteen-story building on Ocean, where we survivors enjoyed sweeping views of the port and the Pacific up and down the coast, living like lords off the huge profits that came with selling the original building.

But the slide continued, and we moved from occupying the entire top floor down to some large offices on the first floor; then back to the 14th floor, half of which we had to sublet. Then, the nadir: back to the first floor into a small office once occupied by three credit union workers.

Was morale down? It was. I had half a desk, which I shared with my new colleague, Rich Archbold, who once had an office the size of your house with a view that stretched from Point Conception to the Mexican border. We grew as close as a married couple, and every bit as vicious, bickering like the Bickertons all day, to the amusement of our dwindling staff.

Then, one day, a couple of entrepreneurs from somewhere else decided to buy the *Orange County Register*, just to our south.

Not only did they buy the paper, but they decided to not fiddle around with the Internet and just concentrate on print, like the glorious olden days. Surely (they must have thought, their minds turned simple from too many years writing greeting cards), people will quit driving cars once they see what a fine wagon they can make.

It was nice to think they could pull it off: Kids on bikes hollering "Paperboy!" as they deftly porched a newspaper that was, as one *Register* exec crowed, "big enough to kill a cat." Be-scissored housewives carefully grooming the supermarket coupons out of the booming Food Section, which would, to stretch out the killing-capacity metaphor, be big enough to kill a medium-size rodent, while Pop checked out the score from his favorite team.

This sweet dream lured some of our remaining talent, not just for the idea, but for more pay.

And not only did these businessmen buy the *Register* and decide to bring back the beautiful past, they set their rosy sights on taking over Long Beach. No doubt they smelled blood, and they should have. We were drenched in it.

They committed three years and millions of dollars to the campaign to run the *Press-Telegram* out of Long Beach.

Engulfed in the bellicose mood, I wrote a perhaps overly bitter column about the "traitors" who left the *Press-Telegram*, which bit of misfortune was spread nationally because all eyes were on the ambitions of the *Register,* with every nostalgia-besotted journalist in the country cheering them on.

Did our morale sink to historic lows (to continue our brutal self-interrogation)? God, no! Our suddenly ruthlessly competitive corporate owners asked us what we needed for the fight. The editors put together a wish list, which, given the times, was a lofty litany of dreams: Maybe some pens. Perhaps some indoor plumbing. The editors actually put together three lists: A "bronze" list of some essentials, a "silver" list of those essentials and a few other baubles, and a "gold" list, which was all kinds of things we wouldn't get: More influence over what we put on the front page (at the time we were basically sharing the front pages with a half-dozen other newspapers that were owned by the same company), maybe a couple of new reporters.

The lists were submitted and summarily rejected. All three of them.

Because we hadn't asked for enough.

Talent ensued. We scored a raft of new reporters, including some of the finest I've ever worked with, and a team of city editors, again including some great ones. I got an unsolicited raise just for standing around.

It was all we needed. In nine months, infused with enthusiasm and pride and probably a very urgent need to kill something, we won the battle in a lot less time than we had girded up for. Within a year of its inaugural issue, the *Long Beach Register* lay dead at our feet like a medium-size rodent that had run afoul of its Food Section.

The war was over, but the world of newspapers, as we had come to know it, was still on its last legs. It's a war we won't win unless print journalism can succeed in reinventing itself and figure out how to wrench the big money of the pre-Internet years in an era where information is both abundant and free.

ANOTHER PIE-IN-THE-SKY PLOT TO KILL GLORIOUS NEWSPRINT

We were reading Wednesday that the hyperfuturistical high-tech company Plastic Logic is getting close to releasing a paper-thin, foldable e-paper tablet.

It's kind of a unique idea with, we imagine, some sort of useful application, but for the most part, we value rigidity in a tablet. If your tablet is paper thin, we're fairly certain that the product's most popular accessory will be some sort of solid slab on which to attach it.

But forget all that. The key point that struck us as we were reading the article about the paper-thin tablet is that the product "could render traditional newspapers and magazines obsolete."

What?! We had to read that a few times. We are, if that sentence proves prescient, doomed.

Everything's been going great in the newspaper business, so why is Plastic Logic sticking its nose into the paper-thin computer idea?

Everybody buys newspapers. Name one person who doesn't subscribe to a newspaper. Yeah, we didn't think you could.

We can't walk down the block without tripping over newspapers in driveways and water puddles. People get up early on Friday morning and wait at the train station for the morning delivery of the paper just to read our Friday Playlist, a weekly compilation of songs selected to fit an appropriate theme.

Do you think we can stroll down any street in this city with any expectation of privacy and not be swarmed by devoted newspaper readers who laugh and cry at our daily offerings in print? We cannot. We're not like you, and we envy you your sweet anonymity that you enjoy as a saddle maker or whatever it is you do.

We are slowly approaching that time in life that people who have soul-sapping jobs happily refer to as retirement.

Our employers will be cheered to know that we have no plans whatsoever to retire. As long as the newspaper business is thriving and robust, we'll be at our typewriter clacking away about our interesting life and what other people are doing wrong with theirs.

But we are concerned, suddenly, about the specter of the obsolescence of traditional newspapers—and our newspaper is absolutely drenched in tradition, going back to the days before its very life was threatened by silent movies and, even more direly, by radio and the damned telegraph.

It is, of course, laughable. Chances are we have nothing to worry about. After all, are we being asked to imagine that one day in the near future the paperboy will be riding his bike up our elm-lined street tossing paper-thin foldable e-paper tablets on our roof?

Plus, we're guessing these things are made out of plastic, or some sort of similar synthetic product that, still, let's face it, is just a fancy word for plastic.

You know what people tell us millions of times each day, no matter how quickly we run to get away from them? They tell us they like the feel of paper. Newsprint, in particular. It's got soul, they say. It's a tactile romance that people have with their newspaper. Plastic Logic will have to peel newspapers from their cold, dead fingers.

As for the other part of that bleak prophecy: that magazines, too, will become obsolete. That's probably true, but who cares? You can always read them online.

CHAPTER NINETEEN

Still Alive! (at Press Time)

Look! I'm still here at the newspaper. Except now our offices are across the street, from, and in the actual shadow of, the old *Press-Telegram* building, the place where I started in 1976, my presence then barely noticeable among the several hundred workers at the five-story plant. Now, on a day when everyone shows up, there's about a dozen of us. It's a small newspaper staff, but a fairly large Internet news staff.

The building that houses the newspaper's writers and editors now is a converted storefront that used to house a sewing-machine shop and, later a Lots O' Lamps store. The 1,200 square-foot room comes with a mezzanine, which is where we store the advertising people, who are going through their own set of techno-changes, trying to monetize the paper's presence on the Internet, especially on mobile devices.

It's how people read the news now, on phones and,

to a lesser degree, on tablet, though the newspaper still comes out every day, as it has for well over 100 years now, in its newsprint analog version. It's read mostly by old people—older than I am, which, you don't need me to tell you, makes for a dwindling market.

Writing for mobile devices takes an entirely new skill set as the online newspaper has mere seconds to capture the reader's interest, and it's even more difficult to hold that elusive interest before it scampers off in any of millions of directions for a fresh source of diversion. Time spent on a particular story is measured in seconds, and it's a mighty compelling story that holds a reader's interest for an entire minute. You might snag a pair of eyes with your first sentence, your bang-up lede; you might hold on to them for the next sentence; by the third, your pair of visiting eyes is starting to wander off the screen; if your fourth sentence isn't a killer, they're off to Candy Crush Saga, Facebook, BuzzFeed, and beyond.

It's a bit easier for a columnist. I've been known to post a story with an average visit time of three minutes which, in cyberjournalism, is huge. And it's because people come to columnists with the intention of reading the whole column. News stories that gather the most readers/views entail murder and other forms of mayhem, and it seems that readers scan it to find out if they recognize the name of whoever's had calamity visited upon them or been the perpetrator of the act. It takes seconds for the reader to become relieved, or perhaps disappointed, that they don't recognize a name, and they move on to the next train wreck.

But with us, readers tend to come for the news about whatever animal has landed in my hair, whatever destruction my dogs have caused, whatever milestone our children are passing, whatever is prompting our outrage. It's not a tremendous amount of people, but it's a devout bunch.

And it's been a pleasure to be allowed to shoot out these daily missives for so long and about so many subjects, from music to politics, to community issues to local and national personalities, to woodpeckers landing on my head (please subsume your urge to make a joke about that. You don't want to come across as tiresomely predictable, do you?), to whatever musing I find amusing when I prance into the old Lots O' Lamps shop each weekday morning.

I look forward to it (almost) every day. At times, I feel like an old bastard, but it's an environment that keeps me thinking, at least, on the youngish side. And the reporters around me, as they've always been, are amazing in their breadth of knowledge. One of the key secrets in journalism is to know a little about a lot of things. You gather enough of these people around you and you have a ton of expertise in dozens of areas: law, theology, government, history, and science all the way down to heraldry, etiquette, and punk rock. We almost don't need Google.

While I've learned about my own past in the course of writing about myself, chiefly in filling in the gaps of my extremely limited knowledge of my mother, my own children won't have to wonder much about their father. It's all been in the paper, and it continues to course around the wires and tubes of the Internet—the very reason I'm dying here.

I feel fine as of this moment while I'm typing this sentence, but it could change sometime in the next paragraph.

A lengthy life-expectancy test I just took on the Internet (which has also replaced doctors) shows me living for twenty-four more years (though none of the questions asked if I just had a series of small strokes). And, when I was asked, while being interviewed by another newspaper a couple of years ago, how much longer I thought newspapers would be around, I said twenty years. That was five years ago, so that gives me fifteen more on (and in) paper.

Then? Nobody knows. Likely, bloggers take over everything, and it will be up to you (and blog-monitoring sites) as to whom you should believe, whom you should trust, whom you enjoy reading. No one like me will be foisted upon you after first slaving away in the salt mines of funeral coverage and Mrs. Senior of Lomita pageants.

A lot of the more reputable and reasoned writing on the Web right now continues to come from writers in the print business. It's outright stolen or otherwise appropriated by aggregators or bloggers who still depend on actual news, as reported by newspaper writers, as a springboard for whatever it is they're blogging about.

More recently, some Internet news sites have been recruiting newspaper writers by offering better pay (for that matter, your local ACE Hardware could offer most newspaper writers better pay). When the newspaper-as-Internet-farm-club dries up, journalism students will, I suppose, go straight from college into Internetting.

There will always, unfortunately, be a lot of white noise of hatred and bellicosity on the Internet, which has moved from desktop computers to mobile devices to eyeglasses to wristwatches in just a few years. There will still be news, and there will still be people who come up through all of that rubble and become respected columnists, if that's the correct terminology for someone who used to fill a literal column of type that ran vertically down one side of a newspaper page.

And those sharers and foisters of opinion people will type away—or more likely chatter into a voice-recognition app—and elucidate, amuse, enrage, and otherwise become a small part of a certain number of people's daily routine, something they'll look forward to each morning and depend on being there forever. Or for at least as long as the extraordinarily lucky writer/chatterer, or the medium itself, is alive.

Acknowledgments

This isn't the book I expected to write and, for that and a hundred other reasons, I have to thank Wendy Thomas Russell and Jennifer Volland, my two brutal and ruthless and totally enjoyable and brilliant editors and publishers who wrassled with my writing like rodeo clowns and kept it from leaping into the crowd to cause calamity and mayhem.

Also appreciated are James Thomas and Jennifer Gravois for their critical readings and for noting certain passages that had perhaps spiraled into depression.

As for everyone else, there are so many names, so many people I've worked with and been close friends with in the newspaper business over the years. I could name a hundred or more and still be guilty of grievous omissions. I can live with that, so a small sampling of people I'll never be able to thank as much as I'd like to include my longtime and ageless boss and colleague Rich Archbold; my dear old friends Dave Wielenga, John Beshears, Dan Winkel, Ruth Ann Karch, Carolyn Ruszkiewicz, Bill Lee Shelton, and Stan Ross Leppard; and, most of all, People Who Know Who They Are.

I couldn't carry on in this life without the current batch of friends and co-workers who continue to pound away at this glorious calling for less money than you'd pay an Uber driver who showed up late and drunk and had his kids in the backseat—especially the fine writers and reporters Josh Dulaney and Andrew Edwards and, even more especially, Melissa Evans, the best city editor I've ever had.

Finally, and as usual, I'm grateful and full of love for my inordinately understanding and caring wife, Jane, and our beautiful children, Ray and Hannah. Plus, whatever dogs we happen to own at the moment.

About the Author

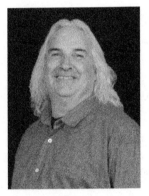

Tim Grobaty, a daily humor columnist at the Long Beach (Calif.) *Press-Telegram*, has won numerous awards, including being named the Best Columnist in the Western United States by Best in the West. He also has authored three books on local history: *Growing Up in Long Beach: Boomer Memories from Autoettes to Los Altos Drive-In; Location Filming in Long Beach;* and *Long Beach Chronicles: From Pioneers to the 1933 Earthquake* (History Press). A native of Long Beach, Grobaty lives (he still lives!) in the city with his wife, daughter, and two pups.

BROWN PAPER PRESS engages readers on topics of contemporary culture through quality writing and thoughtful design. Unbound by genre, our press delivers socially relevant works that advise, guide, inspire, and amuse. We champion authors with new perspectives, strong voices, and original ideas that just might change the world.

For information about new releases, author events, and special promotions, visit **www.brownpaperpress.com**.

**Other books by
Brown Paper Press**

*Relax, It's Just God: How and Why to
Talk to Your Kids About Religion
When You're Not Religious*

*Burdens by Water:
An Unintended Memoir*